JAMES LUCAS AND
JAMES BARKER

THE BATTLE OF NORMANDY

THE FALAISE GAP

HM Holmes & Meier Publishers, Inc.
New York

First published in the United States of America 1978 by
HOLMES & MEIER PUBLISHERS, INC.
30 Irving Place, New York, N.Y. 10003

Library of Congress Cataloging in Publication Data

Lucas, James Sidney.
  The Battle of Normandy, Falaise Gap.

  Bibliography: p. 172
  Includes index
  1. Falaise Gap, Battle of, 1944. I. Barker, James,
joint author. II. Title.
D756.5.F34L8   1978   940.54'21   78-17771
ISBN 0-8419-0418-9

PRINTED IN GREAT BRITAIN

Contents

Illustrations

Maps

Photographs

1 The Allied commanders for 'Operation Overlord'. From left to right Lieut. General C. Hodges, Lieut. General H. Crerar, General Sir Bernard L. Montgomery, Lieut. General Omar Bradley and Lieut. General Sir Miles Dempsey. (*Imperial War Museum*).

2 Lieut. General Omar Bradley and Lieut. General Gerow.

3 Field Marshal Gerd von Rundstedt.

4 Field Marshal Gunther von Kluge.

5 Field Marshal Walther Model.

6 Obergruppenführer Paul Hausser.

7 Field Marshal Erwin Rommel.

8 Oberführer Kurt Meyer, GOC 12th SS Panzer Division.

9 Obersturmbannführer Max Wünsche.

10 Field Marshal Gunther von Kluge in a battlefield conference in Normandy.

11 General der Panzertruppen Geyr von Schweppenburg.

12 Oberstgruppenführer Josef 'Sepp' Dietrich.

13 Shermans of 13/18th Hussars in the bocage shortly after D-Day.

14 Self Propelled artillery of the 1st SS Panzer Division (LSSAH).

15 A Panther and a group of panzergrenadiers crash through a bocage hedge in Normandy.

16 Panzer V, the Panther, in action.

17 An SdKfz 7/1, 8 ton half-track, mounting a 2cm flak. Typical of the light anti-aircraft guns with which the Germans tried to defend their columns against the Allied fighter/bombers.

18 A 3.7cm anti-aircraft gun on an SdKfz 6/2 half-track mounting, here being demonstrated to children (probably not Normandy).

19 German flak troops in training. This is a 2cm flak 30, mounted on an SdKfz 10/4 and capable of use also as an anti-tank weapon.

20 SS panzergrenadiers of a battle group assembling to mount an attack.
21 A company headquarters of an SS panzergrenadier unit waiting for orders to open an attack.
22 Men of an 81mm mortar team.
23 In addition to the anti-tank guns the German anti-tank weapons included rocket launchers such as this Panzerschreck.
24 The strain of battle shows in the faces of these SS Grenadiers. The case slung on the back of the nearer man carried the spare barrel for the machine gun.
25 A machine gun team of Waffen-SS Grenadiers on the Normandy front. The weapon is the fast firing MG 42, here used in an LMG role.
26 A 7.5cm pak camouflaged in a Normandy corn field.
27 & 28 Two aspects of the fighting in Normandy; the confidence of the Allied advance under an air umbrella and German transport with warning signs along the road warning of low flying Allied aircraft and two aircraft spotters.
29 Canadian infantry and armour street fighting in a village on the Falaise road.
30 A Panzer IV, Ausführung H, knocked out during a rearguard action fought against 23rd Hussars of 11th Armoured Division, in Putanges on 18 August, 1944.
31 An assault gun (Sturmgeschütz) mounted on a Panzer III chassis and belonging to the 1st SS Panzer Division pushed into the Orne after it ran out of petrol and had to be abandoned. (*Imperial War Museum*).
32 A Panther of 116th Panzer Division knocked out near St Germain Cathedral in Argentan.
33 A German soft-skinned vehicle column caught and set afire by aerial rocket and machine gun attack in a narrow lane.
34 An aerial shot of the river Dives taken in 1975 and showing in the foreground the Moissy ford. Running from left to right across the picture is the St Lambert–Chambois road. Mount Ormel is just off the picture, top right. (*Courtesy of After the Battle*).
35 An aerial shot of the two bridges across the Dives at St Lambert taken during 1975. These are the two original bridges across which the German troops flooded past the Canadian group under Major Currie. (*Courtesy of After the Battle*).

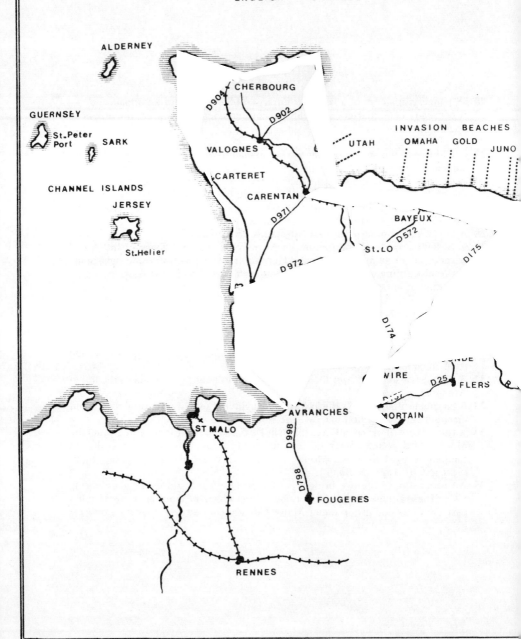

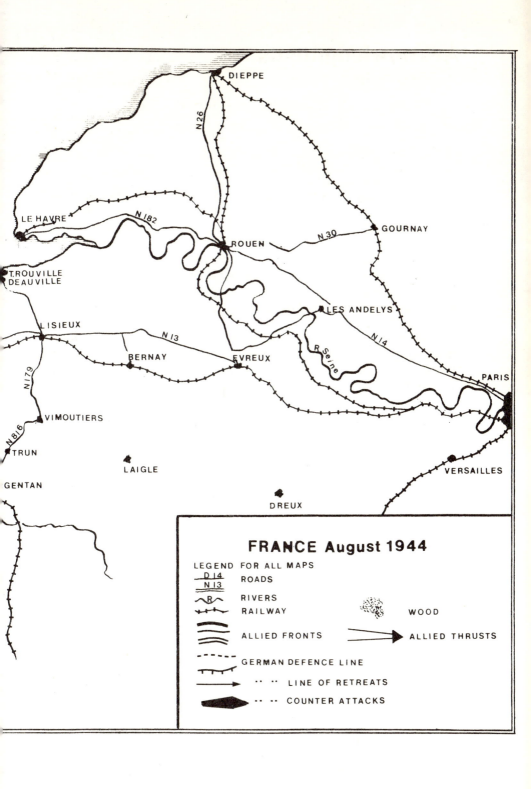

DIEPPE

N 26

LE HAVRE
N 182

GOURNAY
N 30

ROUEN

T.ROUVILLE
DEAUVILLE

LES ANDELYS

LISIEUX
N 13
N 14

BERNAY
EVREUX
R Seine
PARIS

N 179

VIMOUTIERS
N 816

TRUN
LAIGLE

VERSAILLES

GENTAN

DREUX

FRANCE August 1944

LEGEND FOR ALL MAPS
D 14
N 13   ROADS

R   RIVERS

              RAILWAY   WOOD

              ALLIED FRONTS   ALLIED THRUSTS

              GERMAN DEFENCE LINE

              ·· ·· LINE OF RETREATS

              ·· ·· COUNTER ATTACKS

Acknowledgments

In order to achieve coverage from the German side, war diaries, official histories, personal accounts and letters were read and interviews conducted. Some of the details gained are reproduced as extracts while at other places in the text the accounts have been woven into the fabric of the story. There were so many German contributors to our research that it is not possible to list them all and so neither they nor the many institutions who gave us such assistance are mentioned by name. But to them all go our most sincere thanks for the information they gave, and for the photographs which they made available.

On the British side we acknowledge the assistance of the Department of Photographs of the Imperial War Museum, the Public Records Office and the Ministry of Defence (Army) Library. My thanks also to Traude, my wife, to Mary Harris and Barbara Shaw who typed and retyped the manuscript, and to Matthew Cooper for his advice and comments. Some of the photographs in the book are reproduced by permission of the Imperial War Museum and by Winston Ramsey, the editor of the magazine *After the Battle*.

1

BACKGROUND TO
A BATTLE

'Only a battlefield upon which there has been a defeat can surpass in melancholy one upon which a victory has been gained.' WELLINGTON

Introduction

'Our operations in Normandy are rendered exceptionally difficult . . .'
ROMMEL TO OKW, 11 June 1944

Although the battle fought in north-western Europe and given the title of 'Falaise Gap' was of short duration, its antecedents and the planning which was to make possible the encirclement and destruction of the greater part of two German armies during August 1944 was long and intricate.

The first part of this book explains why there was a campaign in north-west Europe and how the situation which led up to the Falaise battle evolved. Within the chapters of the first part some of the commanders who were involved will be described, as well as the tactics which were used and the terrain in which they were employed. Then, in the second part, follow descriptions of the fighting on the western, southern, northern and eastern walls of the Falaise pocket. As a conclusion there is a description of the aftermath of the battle.

The emphasis in this book is more upon the German experience in Normandy than upon the Allied, for their story has already been told in other books. It is the intention to describe here, for the first time in English, the battles in Normandy as experienced by German units.

The reader will appreciate that during the fighting there was on the German side a great deal of confusion and that formations, whether these were large and made up of the remnants of regiments or divisions, or only small groups isolated from their parent bodies, often carried on the fight without central control or direction. To have attempted to describe the actions of each and every German unit or formation would have produced an unnecessarily complicated account. Therefore certain units have been selected to represent the whole. These include 84th Corps, the 1st ss, 9th ss, 10th ss, 12th ss Panzer Divisions and 85th Infantry Division. It is the actions of these formations in attack or defence, in the expectation of victory or in the hopelessness of defeat, which must speak for all the German units which served.

The battle of the Falaise pocket was, for the Germans, a military disaster of the first magnitude. It is our hope that our words do justice and honour the men who were forced to play out that tragedy during the early autumn of 1944.

[This, in outline, is that part of the campaign in France during which the battle of Falaise was fought, from the last day of July to 22 August 1944, in the department of Normandy in France. Battles must be seen as part of the campaign in which they are set.] This vast undertaking was based on Montgomery's revision, in early 1944, of an invasion plan submitted by the Chief of Staff (Designate) to the Supreme Allied Commander (COSSAC) to the Allied combined chiefs of staff in mid-1943, shortly before the former 8th Army commander assumed the post of Allied ground commander for 'Overlord' in early 1944. Montgomery widened the scope of the original plan to include five, instead of three, assault divisions in the first beach landings and three airborne divisions to be dropped on both flanks of the Allied beachhead. The second part of his grand design envisaged a gradual British–Canadian advance to the lower Seine, pivoting on the city of Caen, [while the American armies spread fanwise from Normandy to the deep-water ports along the Brittany and Biscayan coastline above the Loire river, before consolidating and then turning eastwards towards and across the Seine, central and northern France to the borders of Germany.]

On D-Day, Canadian, British and US troops were successful in establishing a sizeable beachhead on the coast of northern France in the Baie de la Seine between Ouistreham at the mouth of the River Orne in the east and Les Dunes de Varraville beyond the Vire estuary in the west. Using air power to ham-string road, rail, waterway and sea communications throughout western Europe, and deception strategy to pin down German forces throughout the Reich's still-massive land empire, the Allies were able to prevent the Germans from rushing their reserves to Normandy, particularly the 18 infantry divisions held in the Pas de Calais where an invasion had always been expected. Meanwhile, the panzer formations in von Rundstedt's command – the élite of the German forces in the west – were drawn into static fighting around Caen against Montgomery's 21st Army. Largely unsupported by infantry, they had no time in which they could rest, re-group and take part in their intended role of providing the core of a counter-attack force which would sweep the Allies into the Channel.

Thus, while the main strength of the German armour had been lured to, and held on, the British sector (there to prevent a break-out by the Canadians towards the Seine and Paris), the 1st US Army was left free to expand its bridgehead on either side of the Vire estuary and, eventually, to occupy the Cotentin peninsula, the capture of whose principal town, the port of Cherbourg, was seen as essential to the maintenance of a secure foothold in Europe.

With this first phase of Operation Overlord, the invasion of France, successfully completed the Allied armies embarked upon the second and subsequently more controversial stage of the campaign, the break-out into the heart of France. Hitler's orders to his armies that not an inch of territory was to be yielded ultimately benefited the Allies and ensured defeat for the German troops defending Normandy. Nevertheless, the stubborn German defence, together with the eminent suitability of the Norman countryside for close combat and small-scale defensive engagements slowed the pace of the Allies' advance and caused them heavy losses in return for minor territorial gains. The US forces were affected particularly badly. Because of temperament and training they found the bitter and unrelenting struggle in the close-set fields and hedgerows of the bocage country hard to bear. The slow pace of this advance led to dissatisfaction with the progress of the campaign and to criticism of the Allied ground commander, Montgomery. Such ill-informed, inaccurate judgments ignored the fact that the German commanders were being compelled to react to his strategy. Many of the delays which beset the Allies in those first few weeks and which had upset the time-table organized by SHAEF were due to the difficulty the divisions of Bradley's 1st Army had in overcoming the defences of 7th German Army and then of fighting their way forward to establish a firm line from which an eventual break-out could be made. Not until 19 July was this position reached when after bitter fighting, which occasioned them heavy losses, the Americans captured St Lô.

The succeeding week on 1st US Army's front was the calm before the storm, brought about by the need to re-group, to bring up reinforcements and by the restrictions placed by bad weather on aerial sorties. Opposite Panzer Group West's front around Caen, a series of British offensives had appeared to have failed, provoking anxiety at SHAEF and in the British and US press. Montgomery's standing was thus undermined; Eisenhower's own loss of confidence in the British commander's handling of the campaign at this stage of the north-west European fighting was to play an important part in his decision to assume direct and personal control of ground operations on 1 September 1944.

Although 'Goodwood', the largest and most ambitious of these British offensives, had failed in its stated purpose of breaching the German defences south of Caen, it had nevertheless brought the Germans to the point of collapse in Normandy, reducing their senior commanders like Field Marshal von Kluge to despair. Thus, paradoxically, the volume of criticism directed at Montgomery rose to a climax just at the time – the last week of July – when his direction of the campaign had finally unbalanced his German opponents, allowing the Allied armies in the four weeks which followed to reap the reward for the hard-fought battles which had been their lot since D-Day.

Eisenhower's command reshuffle on 1 August re-organized the Allied armies into two Army Groups. Bradley's 12th US contained the 1st and 3rd US armies while Montgomery's British and Canadian 21st Army Group comprised 2nd British Army and 1st Canadian Army. As a result of this arrangement Bradley now enjoyed equal status with Montgomery, although operational direction and the supervision of tactical co-ordination between the two Allied army groups was retained by the British commander. This state of affairs gave Bradley a greater measure of control over the American troops at that stage of the campaign when divergent views, chiefly along national lines, were beginning to manifest themselves in the strategic considerations on the future conduct of the campaign.

The seeds of inter-Allied misunderstanding and friction were sown by developments on 3rd US Army front. The break-out by Patton's forces into Brittany met with only minimal resistance and made such good ground that both he and the more adventurous of his divisional commanders began to consider prospects more alluring than those envisaged in 'Overlord's' concept of a planned, gradual and well-supplied advance from the Brittany and Biscayan deep-water ports through France to the German frontier. In their pursuit of weakening German opposition the tank spearheads of 3rd US Army were drawn away from the Atlantic along the southern flank of 7th German Army and thus southwards and eastwards towards the Loire and Seine. While Patton's men raced eastwards into the interior of France, the British and Canadian armies were still largely being held around Caen – fulfilling even at this last stage of the campaign Montgomery's original intention that they should pin down the bulk of the German armour.

From D-Day until 25 July 1944 the deployment of the two German armies reflected the separate approaches of their commanders to the problem of defending different kinds of terrain, with a wide disparity of strength distinguishing 7th Army from its more bountifully kitted-out partner, Panzer Group West. Conventional military wisdom, from Hitler downwards, dictated the need to keep the right wing facing the British and Canadians around Caen strong in order to prevent a break-out aimed directly at Paris and the heart of France. The GOC of Panzer Group West had established a front consisting of a shallow defensive line which consisted of thinly-held outposts and main lines of resistance. Echeloned deep behind the defensive lines and the anti-tank artillery were panzer and infantry battle-groups; behind them sited deeply in Panzer Group West's front were the panzer divisions themselves, grouped in an operational reserve ready to seal off British penetrations. Eberbach, who replaced Geyr von Schweppenburg as the commander of Panzer Group West on 4 July 1944, was fortunate that the Luftwaffe's 3rd Flak Corps, the finest anti-tank unit available *anywhere* in the west, was placed under his command. Ideally, both he and his predecessor should have employed more standard infantry formations but, for reasons which will become clear much later in this book, none were deemed available to relieve his overworked and tired panzers in the crucial early weeks of June and for much of July.

The 7th Army facing the Americans had easier terrain to defend and could hold its position with fewer men. In view of the priority placed on bolstering Panzer Group West's front, this was a definite advantage. Waffen-SS General Hausser (GOC 7th Army from 28 June 1944) grouped his reserves behind a thin screen of infantry and reinforced them with self-propelled artillery which, to compensate for the scarcity of tanks, were available in large numbers. Although such AFVs lacked turrets, both their armour protection and fire-power were superior to those of the M4 Shermans which were their main protagonists in the US armoured battalions. Nevertheless, while 7th Army had three fresh infantry divisions and certain composite units and 'Kampfgruppen' with which it could bolster its defences, for some weeks it was bereft of the support of even a single panzer division. Of those armoured formations that came its way, some had already suffered heavy losses on Panzer Group West's sector, while others invariably had to detach battle-groups to relieve first Schweppenburg and then Eberbach's command in its frequent moments of crisis, leaving them perilously below full-strength.

Behind their relatively short line based in good defensive country where their fighting skills largely cancelled out the Allies' material superiority, the German armies in Normandy managed to keep their enemies confined in a narrow beachhead until late July, when 'Operation Cobra' fatally ruptured 7th Army's front.

Even after 'Cobra', it would have been possible for the Germans to have cut their losses in Normandy and make a reasonably organized withdrawal to the Seine, with a high proportion of Army Group 'B' intact and in good order. But then Hitler, unexpectedly and disastrously, intervened. At the beginning of August 1944, a large sack was beginning to form around the two German armies, with Patton's 3rd US Army racing round 7th Army's fragmented south-western and southern flanks and with Montgomery's 21st Army Group on 5th Panzer Army's sector in the north and north-west preparing to crack the German front along its entire length with the aim of capturing Falaise. Blithely ignoring these potentially catastrophic developments, Hitler presented the Allies with the opportunity of accomplishing the encirclement and the destruction of his armies while they were still in Normandy by ordering an offensive, code-named 'Operation Liège', against the Americans from Mortain. The initial intention was to capture Avranches and thus to close the gap at the base of the Cotentin peninsula through which Patton's forces were streaming. The German thrust was then to strike northwards to drive back the Americans into the sea. The Mortain offensive rested upon three absurd premises. The first of these was that Patton's advance could be halted by the seizure of Avranches, a move which would cut off the US armoured spearheads from their supplies. The second, equally unlikely premise, was that the Americans would not fight well against a German offensive. The third was Hitler's prophecy that bad weather during the crucial opening moments of the offensive would keep the Allies' fighter-bombers grounded, unable to intervene – a prognostication which fell apart as soon as British and US aircraft began to savage the Germans' panzer and supply columns on the very morning of the attack.

The seizure of Avranches, when viewed on a large-scale map at Hitler's

17

headquarters at Rastenburg in East Prussia, seemed easily within the capabilities of the forces in that sector. The distance to the objective seemed small and the divisions gathered for the operation seemed to be sufficiently strong to carry out this task. But the local commanders knew how tired were the understrength panzer divisions of Kluge's Army Group. Most of the formations involved had been fighting without much relief since late June and, if ground was gained in the opening stages of the offensive their shattered remnants would be physically incapable of holding it indefinitely. Even if the attack had sufficient strength to reach Avranches it could never carry out the rest of Hitler's ambitious plan to strike northwards and a resealing of the base of the peninsula could, at best, be only a temporary expedient. It was clear to the senior commanders of the two German armies in Normandy that the Mortain offensive was doomed to fail even before it had begun. Nor was this pessimism confined only to the senior commanders; Graf von Schwerin, commander of the 116th Panzer Division, refused to allow his formation to move forward to the attack and was replaced for his insubordination.

The launching of the Mortain offensive did not affect the dashing pace of 3rd US Army's advance. On 10 August, its 15th Corps drove northwards from Le Mans, aiming for Alençon and then Argentan, where Montgomery had planned that it would link with the Canadians coming down from the north. The pocket between Falaise and Argentan was now beginning to take perceptible shape. But at this point, delays were encountered on 21st Army Group's front. Although depleted through constant fighting and the requirements of 'Operation Liège', the German forces opposite the 2nd British and 1st Canadian Armies were able to blunt their progress. Due to their determined resistance, Falaise – the northern gate of the pocket – did not fall until 16 August.

In the meantime, 15th US Corps' advance on the southern flank was stopped, for several reasons. Part of the corps was despatched to the Seine in accordance with Bradley's compliance with a directive of Montgomery's which anticipated a second, even greater, encirclement along the west bank of the lower Seine. Only a rump of 15th Corps was left in position, a rump which was too weak to close the ring around the German armies at Argentan. The point where the Allied armies were to link up was then shifted from Argentan north-eastwards to the village of Chambois.

Having at last overcome the German defences covering Falaise and the Dives valley, the Poles and Canadians advancing from the north-east linked up with the Americans on 19 and 20 August. With the destruction of the pocket, the two-and-a-half month old campaign in Normandy came to an end. These last German troops to be killed or captured were thus despatched on 22 August.

German rear-guards made their way across the Seine on 29 and 30 August. Behind them in the Falaise area and at the Seine crossing points they had left nearly all their heavy equipment and transport. In the pocket itself, the casualties included 2,000 dead horses, with 3,000 more found alive. Ten thousand soldiers had been killed in action and 40,000 more taken prisoner. But more than 50,000 had managed to escape from the pocket, led by their army, corps and divisional commanders who had, by and large, kept their heads in circumstances which, in the latter days, were nothing short of apocalyptic.

In defence of the Allied commanders' failure fully to exploit the German predicament, neither Montgomery nor Bradley was aware that so many German formations were still west of the Falaise-Argentan line when the confusion over the inter-army group boundaries around Argentan took place between 13 and 16 August; had they known, they would have acted accordingly and the German defeat, crushing as it was, would have been complete. No one on the Allied side at any time during this period (8–22 August) was able to estimate the number of German troops in the pocket with any degree of accuracy. [The collapse had been so sudden and so complete that normal sources of intelligence, such as wireless transmission intercepts and captured documents – all of which hold good when the enemy forces retain their tactical cohesion – lost their value as German divisions were reduced to isolated groups often of only company strength, fighting little wars of their own outside the control of higher echelons.]

In all, the German Army had lost over 300,000 men killed, wounded and missing since D-Day. In their retreat from France, they left another 100,000 troops invested in ports along the Biscayan and Channel coasts and in the Channel Isles. Allied losses of 220,000, of which 37,000 were fatal, were proof of the ferocity of the fighting in Normandy and indicative of the price which attacking armies have to pay in assaulting well-sited and tenacious defenders. There are no precise figures for civilian losses during the months in which Normandy was turned into a battlefield. Ten thousand dead is a conservative estimate. The price of liberation for the Norman and Breton provinces was a ravaged countryside, devastated towns and villages, destroyed antiquities, wrecked railways and public utilities. Now it was all over, the Allies, securely established on the mainland of Europe, could begin to prepare for the final stage of the war – the invasion of Germany.

The Allied Effort

'We have a special relationship . . .'

Two important factors with regard to the world balance of power emerged during the course of the Second World War. The first was that, with the collapse of the major continental European powers through German conquest from 1939–41, and thereafter with the approach of defeat for Hitler's Germany and her Axis partners, the immediate post-war world would become the preserve of the three major Allied powers; the United States of America, Great Britain and the Soviet Union. The second was that Britain, lacking either of her two great allies' economic and military muscle, would have to sacrifice some of her political interests in favour of those of her closest partner in the war-time alliance – the United States – owing to her dependence on the latter for war-aid. Churchill's latent recognition of this state of affairs was tempered by a deep affection and respect for his American ally; nevertheless, they were sentiments which did not prevent either him or his team of experienced political and military leaders from occasionally disagreeing sharply, even acrimoniously, with their US counterparts during the course of the many lengthy inter-Allied conferences and committee meetings.

As the war moved towards its close, so Britain drew more heavily on her well-nigh exhausted human and economic reserves, subverting Churchill's efforts to get Roosevelt to pressurise Stalin into accepting the kind of post-war settlement which would prevent a German military occupation of Eastern Europe being exchanged for an equally harsh and more permanent Soviet one. The US president was aware of his nation's rise to world-power status and also of his British ally's relative decline, but was not as astute as Churchill in matters of foreign and strategic policy, and certainly not as realistic as the British leader in his assessment of the nature of Soviet Russia's war aims and the difficulties that these would contribute in the establishment of a working post-war European settlement. The reasons for Roosevelt's innocence in the realm of foreign policy need not further detain us but, as Churchill believed it to be vitally necessary to integrate the western Allies' war-time strategy more closely to a peace-time settlement in their – and not Stalin's – favour, the durable nature of this particular characterisation, even when it ran up against the British Prime Minister's greater experience, was to have a crucial bearing on the conduct of Allied strategy from 1943 onwards.

The American president's attitude towards his British ally was occasionally one of suspicion and mistrust, influenced by his understanding and interpretation of Britain's traditional manner of waging war which he saw as imperialist. Both he and his advisers were reluctant to risk American lives in what they saw as entirely British military adventures aimed solely at securing the British Empire. This resolve hardened first when they were faced with Churchill's plans to prosecute the war against the Axis powers by indirect approach through the Mediterranean and the Balkans, and then from 1943 onwards when the US contribution to the ETO, massively increased, dwarfed the British efforts.

The alliance between the United States and Great Britain had been cemented by personal meetings between Roosevelt and Churchill following a close and private correspondence which had begun between them in 1939 when Churchill became First Lord of the Admiralty. The first of these personal conferences at supreme level had taken place in Placentia Bay, Newfoundland in August 1941, while America was still at peace with the Axis powers. At this meeting the two leaders put their names to the only public declaration of Allied war aims which they were to make, other than the 'unconditional surrender' statement, and this 1941 declaration, in which the basic human freedoms were specified, has become known as the Atlantic Charter.

There were to be eight other occasions before the invasion of France on which the two war leaders met to thrash out strategic policies, and the conference at which Operation Overlord, the invasion intention, was finally and almost unreservedly accepted by the British, was held during August 1943 at Quebec.

The north-west Europe campaign of which Operation Overlord was the opening manoeuvre was occasioned by the fact that Germany had been in occupation of the greater part of Europe since 1941. Only Sweden, Spain, Switzerland and Portugal had not been invaded by the Wehrmacht. Until 6 June 1944 the only active British and US contribution to the war against the territory of the Third Reich had been of a peripheral nature, namely a round the clock bombing offensive against German industries and cities which, although unsuccessful in its strategic intent of crippling war-production and civilian morale, had nevertheless distorted the growth of German industry and had led to the diversion of resources and manpower to counter the massive, Allied continental air offensive. On land, following the defeat of the Axis forces in Africa and in Sicily, there had been a tying down of German divisions in Italy and at sea a successful but not absolute reduction of Germany's surface and submarine fleets.

Yet all these achievements were of little significance compared to the great mission which the Allies undertook in the summer of 1944. Operation Overlord was accepted with varying degrees of enthusiasm by US and British statesmen and military commanders as being the only valid war-winning strategy which would finally bring about the opening of the Second Front and provide the means for the destruction of the German armies in France and the Low Countries, from whence an invasion of the Reich itself could be launched.

Had this enterprise not been entered upon at that time then the introduction of certain German secret weapons would certainly have meant an indefinite prolongation of the war and set-backs and disaster for the Allied cause. Yet Operation Overlord was a step which the Allies were reluctant to take. Its undertaking, even at that late stage of the war, required on their part a steeling of nerves, for they felt that their massive accumulation of troops, weapons and equipment, their mastery of the skies and a comprehensive range of successful stratagems might still prove insufficient to guarantee a favourable issue. Such was the respect they had for their adversary.

Of the two Allies Great Britain had had the greater experience of fighting the German war machine and was more reluctant to take on the Wehrmacht in strength in north-west Europe, preferring an indirect and attritive strategy. Since 1940 the British land-fighting against Germany had been restricted to the Mediterranean theatre and, for the greater part of those years, in Africa. The majority of the troops serving in the Middle East, a long-standing British sphere of influence, came from the United Kingdom and from the British Empire, and a good deal of their equipment was either produced locally or in the Imperial territories. Given these facts it is not surprising that, following the entry of the United States into the war at the end of 1941, Churchill sought to maintain the Mediterranean as the principal theatre of operations against the Axis Powers.

The entry of the United States into the war brought an immediate change of emphasis into the search for a single Allied strategy. Roosevelt and his military and political planners, assuming that their country might eventually provide the major share of the Allies' contribution to the war againnst Germany were, therefore, anxious to influence the British to accept their own ideas on strategy and on the prosecution of the war. The most pressing need, as the Americans saw it, was to take on some of the burden which the Red Army had been carrying since the summer of 1941. In the view of the United States' planners this relief could only come by opening, without delay, a second front in Europe which would draw off German divisions from the east.

The Americans reacted with suspicion to British proposals for a Mediterranean strategy, for in their political naïvety they suspected that the British were more concerned with a possible post-war expansion of their Empire than with prosecuting the war against Nazi Germany. The Americans were without recent and first-hand experience of the ability of the German Army and were unable to understand the reluctance of the British to undertake an immediate campaign in north-west Europe against this strong and potent enemy. Surely, they argued, such an operation would speedily bring the war to a successful close.

Certain that a high casualty rate would be the concomitant of an ill-planned and weak expedition to France the British offered to the Americans again the alternative of the indirect strategy which would eventually weaken the Germans and prepare them for the killing thrust, but the US planners remained unconvinced and proposed two military cross-Channel attacks, Operation Roundup and Operation Sledgehammer. 'Roundup', to be launched in 1942, called for two amphibious landings to be made near Calais and Dieppe by a force of from four to eight divisions, while 'Sledgehammer', the plan for 1943, was to be an assault by eight to ten divisions on the Cotentin peninsula near to Cherbourg. Had these plans been carried through by the Allies with the scanty resources available at that time, then the result would have been so great a disaster that a successful re-entry into Europe might have been postponed for years.

Churchill and his advisers viewed with alarm and disbelief the over-optimistic American plans for victory in 1942 and eventually brought the US planners round to their own view that a premature and failed landing would be a blood-bath. The two operations 'Roundup' and 'Sledgehammer' were shelved. As if to underline the British arguments against the danger of unplanned and hasty operations the Canadian assault upon Dieppe during August 1942 failed disastrously. The human and material losses in this assault were proof of the need to overcome the tactical problems which accompany the landing of an army from ships on to beaches defended by a determined and alerted enemy occupying well-fortified positions.

The impact on Allied military policy-making of the 'reconnaissance in force' at Dieppe was a brutal but very necessary one. Some Americans suspected that Churchill had relied upon the Dieppe operation failing totally in order to convince the restless and brashly confident US ally that it would be folly to launch a cross-Channel attack during 1942. If true a set-back willingly courted at that time and on a comparatively minor scale was preferable to a massive disaster at some later date.

The 22-month delay between the raid on Dieppe and the first day of the invasion of France was largely the product of hold-ups in the production of the specialized equipment required to transport a mass Army across the Channel. Although most of the equipment was British designed on the lessons learnt at Dieppe, the industrial capacity of the United Kingdom had been stretched to the limit by 1943 and the construction had to be carried out in US shipyards and factories. Some American officers expressed the view that much of the specialized equipment was unnecessary and the US Army, with a largely untested belief in its ability to fight its way ashore, turned down the offer of British-made, specially designed tanks in favour of older and, as it turned out, costlier methods. The 2,000 American casualties on Omaha beach were the victims of this example of American insularity of thought.

23

By the end of 1942 the mobilized American war industry was attaining levels of production which made it possible to supply with military equipment not only its own expanding army but also in part those of the USSR and of the British Empire. An ever-increasing variety of US-made weapons and equipment was supplied to the Allies and the prodigious American industrial effort could not but undermine the British influence in the conduct of the Allied war effort. It was against this backdrop and that of a generally improved war situation that the heads of the British and American military authorities met at Casablanca in January 1943. Their task, to thrash out a common strategy. Although Marshall and his team came to the conference table determined to make the British accept proposals for a cross-Channel invasion during 1943, the more experienced British were able to influence their American partners by bringing to the conference the principal experts from Churchill's headquarters and all the relevant information to back their arguments.

Two US observers wrote:

> They [the British] swarmed down upon us like locusts, with a plentiful supply of planners and various other assistants, with prepared plans to ensure that they not only accomplished their purpose but that they did so in stride and with a fair promise of continuing their role of directing, strategically, the course of the War. . . . It was clear that we were confronted by generations of experience in committee work and in rationalizing points of view. . . . In matters touching the European theatre the British had a 100% airtight, hermetically sealed monopoly on intelligence about the enemy. They were the sole and unquestioned authority, firstly, because we had no military intelligence on the continent worthy of the name and secondly, because the British had, and an excellent one too.

The British at Casablanca came away with most of their plans accepted. It was agreed that following the defeat of Doenitz's U-boats and the destruction of the Axis armies in Africa; would come an invasion of Sicily, the undermining of the Axis hold in the Balkans, the final collapse of Italian military power and the end of Turkish neutrality through the reinforcement of the Allied military presence in the Mediterranean. Meanwhile, in the United Kingdom, there would be a rapid build-up of US forces in preparation for the invasion of Europe during the spring of 1944 as well as an intensification of a 'campaign of political warfare, subversion, economic warfare and deception in order to undermine the German will and ability to fight and to pin down his forces wherever they might be found'.

Nevertheless Roosevelt's will prevailed in one vital, political matter whose import thereafter was greater than all the other decisions reached at Casablanca. Having lost the military argument the American President was determined to regain the political advantage and at the end of the Casablanca conference, without consulting either his British ally or even his own military advisers, he suddenly announced that it was the intention of the Allies to press for the unconditional surrender of Germany, Italy and Japan.

It now appeared to the bulk of the populations of those countries that the Allies were determined to crush them utterly and the propaganda instruments of the Axis Powers played upon those fears. There was now nothing for the people but to fight to a finish. With his two words 'unconditional surrender' blurted out almost by accident, Roosevelt strengthened the resolve of the peoples of Germany and Japan and undoubtedly lengthened the war. In his own way the American President was echoing his preference, as well as that of his own military and political circle, for adopting simple slogans as the basis of US policy. The British did not have this mental inflexibility for they were more experienced in international negotiation and thus more able to reach practical solutions to complicated issues.

Temperamentally, the leading personalities of the Anglo-American alliance were, on occasions, poorly matched but a native good sense on both sides and the overriding needs of the moment did not allow this fact to assume too great a significance.

In conclusion, it must be said that many historians in examining the relations which existed between the United States and Great Britain over the years from 1942 to 1945, focus more attention than is deserved upon the arguments and suspicions that were traded between those nations at the highest levels of government and command. Such subjective analysis tends to ignore the very simple and obvious fact that it is difficult to achieve complete agreement between two Powers, even where these share a common language, philosophical and political traditions. Even those bonds proved insufficient to obscure the vast differences in outlook and temperament between the Anglo-Saxon Powers. One suspects that the reputation which the ordinary American has for generosity and friendliness, together with the self-proclaimed idealism of successive US presidential administrations and a belief in the 'special relationship' that supposedly exists between Great Britain and America, has not prepared the British people to absorb the fact that the Americans drove a hard bargain with Britain during the war. Lend-Lease was not a charity, nor was it entirely a one-way process, as Dorothy Crisp points out in her book *The Dominance of England*. It would have been inconceivable that such massive US economic and military assistance would have been given without some definite *quid pro quo* arrangement and naïve to think that the Americans would not place their own interests before ours.

Given the tremendous disparity in strength that emerged between Britain and America the assertion of the latter's power and influence upon the former was both inevitable and unavoidable. Britain could have had no better war-time ally than the United States, and when it is considered how close was Allied co-operation in such vital, technical areas as radar and tank production and the development and production of the first atomic bomb, to say nothing of Allied global strategy, then the surprise is that agreement was reached without rancour upon a wide variety of war-time objectives.

The Growth of Allied Invasion Plans

Throughout the middle years of the war when the Anglo-American command structure was slowly assembled, the invasion of north-west Europe was first deliberated and then planned. The first step was taken in January 1942, with the formation in Washington of the Combined Chiefs of Staff Committee which consisted of the newly created US Joint Chiefs of Staff Committee and a British delegation. The unrelenting American pressure to force the British to accept the opening of a second front in northern France during 1942 led to the establishment of a further committee to consider the merits and demerits of the American-inspired Operation Sledgehammer. This committee, made up of the three British Service Chiefs who had been selected to command the projected expedition, remained in being even when a larger Anglo-American planning organisation COSSAC (Chief of Staff to the Supreme Allied Commander), was formed in London following the Casablanca conference. Headed by a British nominee, General Morgan, and with an American Chief of Staff COSSAC's brief included the need to devise deception stratagems which would convince OKW that the Allies meant to land on the Pas de Calais during the summer of 1943. A second task was to plan for a sudden Allied landing in France in the event of a rapid German withdrawal from Western Europe, and thirdly it was to plan for the eventuality that a coup against Hitler would succeed. The possibility of these latter alternatives had become known to British Intelligence and contingency plans drawn up to exploit any situation. The fourth, and last, term of reference for the committee was to lay out the planning foundation for a full-scale invasion of the European continent in 1944. It then had to select a suitable landing zone along the French coast, devise the theoretical means through which such an undertaking could be supplied and lay down the tactical guidelines for the assault and for its development, once a lodgement area had been carved out COSSAC officers had the initial task of marrying British and American committee procedures, for these were initially bedevilled by differences in terminology.

The failure of the landing at Dieppe in 1942 produced new problems to be resolved. The Allied planners would have to study more deeply the techniques of sea-borne landings and to devise tactics which would enable an army to be landed on a hostile shore without suffering crippling losses. To prepare the Allies for the invasion of Europe further research was ordered into the construction of large landing craft and more powerful close support vessels. Special armoured fighting vehicles were designed to assist in the demolition of the coastal fortifications and in the surmounting of beach obstacles. Tanks which could swim ashore under their own power were built. Finally, the basic tactical lessons learned from the mistakes at Dieppe were analysed and absorbed.

COSSAC drew up its plans in an atmosphere of considerable uncertainty as Churchill was still hoping to avoid an irrevocable commitment to much of the enterprise and used the fluid situation prevailing in the Mediterranean, following Italy's capitulation in September 1943, to obtain Roosevelt's consent to further Anglo-American military actions in that theatre. By March 1944, COSSAC had bequeathed to its successor SHAEF a wide-ranging but incomplete set of proposals upon which more detailed and comprehensive planning could be carried out. One of its committees, under the chairmanship of Lord Louis Mountbatten, selected the area of northern France upon which the Allies would debark, while others considered the design and production of the equipment which would facilitate the landing and subsequent build-up operations.

The task of SHAEF was to bring all those plans and ideas together into a master plan from which Overlord would be implemented. Its chief, Eisenhower, and his Chief of Staff, Bedell Smith, were American but there was a great dependence upon British experience. The deputy to the Supreme Commander was Air Chief Marshal Tedder. Serving under those three men were Admiral Ramsay, Air Chief Marshal Leigh-Mallory, General Bradley and General Montgomery, whose role of ground commander as well as commander of 21st Army Group was seen to be crucial to the success of the operation.

As a result of the increase in numbers of American troops in the United Kingdom during the latter half of 1943 and the early months of 1944, the accumulation of specialized equipment and the maturing of Allied deception plans and cover stratagems, SHAEF was in a better position to reach decisions on the methods which would be used to carry out the invasion. In the light of the US demand for an invasion of north-west Europe it is surprising to discover that one difficulty which faced the Overlord planners was the American decision to launch an invasion of southern France (Operation Anvil) concurrently with the main landing in Normandy. As there was a shortage of landing craft in Europe preparations for Anvil placed an additional and well-nigh unbearable strain upon the committee. Technical arguments on the carrying capacity of the available vessels were factors which soured the otherwise harmonious relations between the Allies. Then in April 1944 there was an unexpected set-back when the US Navy lost two tank landing ships and suffered heavy damage to five more as a result of a raid by German motor torpedo boats during a rehearsal by American amphibious forces off the coast of Dorset. The result of this raid left the Allies with no reserves of tank landing craft for Overlord. Operation Anvil had therefore to be postponed until August.

The Allied Armies

The composition of the American and British armies in the Normandy campaign in terms of the balance between infantry, artillery and armour reflected tactical lessons learnt by both partners during the first half of the war integrated with older modes of tactical organization.

The immediate Allied response to the German victory of 1940 was to set about the task of raising armoured divisions similar in organization and strength to those of the 1940-pattern, German panzer divisions who were given the task of breaking through an enemy front and of carving deep into his lines of communication. The British and the Americans remained loyal, however, to the theory of tanks being used in the support of infantry and the British went so far as to inegrate a three-battalion tank brigade with an infantry division which had been reduced in establishment to two infantry brigades, each of three battalions in place of the standard three brigades. Experiences in several theatres of operation proved this to be a tactically unsound formation, for such a unit lacked infantry strength.

By contrast the German experience had led to the formation of *Kampfgruppen* (battle groups) smaller in size than a division and usually with equal proportions of armour, artillery and infantry, the whole acting in a well-directed and co-ordinated fashion. The Allies, and particularly the British, were less successful in combining the three separate arms of service in anything less than divisional 'set-piece' strength. The composition of the 1944-pattern US armoured division, where the organisation was admittedly incomplete, allowed for a more flexible deployment of its 300 tanks and 12,000 men than its British counterpart consisting of 380 tanks and 15,000 men.

The Americans formed the hard edge of their armoured divisions in three combat commands each of which contained a tank battalion, a motorised infantry battalion, a self-propelled artillery unit and a tank-destroyer squadron. Each combat command had a component of signals, engineers and other services and each was capable of independent action, although they more usually operated as a whole.

In Normandy the early British experience of infantry–tank collaboration was not altogether a happy one, probably because of regimental traditions and a difference in attitudes between the tankmen and the infantry. Then, as a result of the close fighting in the Normandy bocage, a mixed brigade system was introduced. A tank battalion was paired with an infantry battalion and two of these groups formed the mixed brigade. This arrangement proved to be successful in fighting against the German tank-killer teams equipped with their *Panzerfaust* and *Panzerschreck* rocket launchers.

It remains true, however, that the Western Allies never achieved the success which the Germans enjoyed in forming *ad hoc* groups, often no more than of company strength, which could wreak such havoc in the confines of the Normandy countryside.

The US and British infantry formations retained their three-brigade/ regiment structure more or less intact, but through the addition of more powerful anti-tank and anti-aircraft guns dramatically increased their fire power over that with which they had begun the war. Within the rifle battalions, light machine guns, machine pistols, mortars and infantry anti-tank weapons were increased in number. There, too, new weapons strengthened the infantry arm and PIATS (Projector Infantry Anti-Tank) and bazookas, in the British and in the American Army respectively. The peculiar ground conditions of the Norman countryside soon showed that the determined infantryman, concealed in the dense hedgerows could contain an armoured attack using only close-range anti-tank weapons and thus the infantryman was restored to his former pre-eminence, since the Normandy campaign was essentially an infantry war in which air power, armour and artillery were often at a discount.

The British laid great stress on the power of artillery and developed this throughout the war. Both Allied armies possessed special large groupings of artillery units which were distributed usually by army to a corps or, indeed, to divisions when it became necessary to supplement the already powerful artillery force on the divisional establishment. These formations of artillery (the British called them Army Groups Royal Artillery) were of approximate brigade strength and contained field, medium and heavy artillery regiments (battalions in American terminology). In the early days of the Normandy bridgehead and, later, in the Falaise 'pocket' it was possible to co-ordinate the artillery groupings of both Allied armies in a concentration of fire upon selected targets.

The Germans in comparison were badly supplied with artillery pieces, and air supremacy of the Allies forced German dumps to be located a long way behind the front line. In place of heavy artillery the Germans used the heavy and super-heavy mortars (*Nebelwerfer*) whose psychological effect was out of all proportion to the casualties they caused. German battalions were well supplied with light, mobile, accurate mortars; British medical teams calculated that 80 per cent of the casualties in Normandy were due to the effect of standard mortar fire.

The British Army

Most of the soldiers who fought in Normandy were conscripts. The Canadians, on the other hand, were all volunteers. Both armies, however, suffered from a shortage of infantry which was to lead to severe difficulties later in the north-west European campaign.

The burden of the fighting was borne by an infantry arm which had shrunk to only fourteen per cent of the military whole and to whom there were given neither supplements of pay nor special insignia to distinguish their special skills. The bewildering complexity of twentieth-century warfare – the products of mechanization, the introduction of new weapons and all the mass of equipment required to keep the twentieth-century man in uniform fed, in good health and in good morale – led to what Correlli Barnett has termed the civilianization of the military profession, of which the growth of the Army's 'tail' was its most striking feature. No less than forty-four per cent of 21st Army Group's manpower was made up of Service troops and the remaining forty-two per cent contained the artillery, the Engineers and the armoured formations.

The soldiers were better educated and better informed than those of the First World War. They were less inclined to accept things on trust, had a greater tendency to answer back and were more insistent on knowing the reason why they should risk their lives for a military objective. As a consequence:

> The men of the Second World War did not show the same qualities of stoical endurance as those of the Great War. Divisions lost their 'attacking edge' more quickly. A lower proportion of casualties than in the Great War was needed to bring a unit to the point of needing relief. This was the prize paid for higher effective intelligence and initiative – for social progress.

Faced with invading a Continent defended by tried and tested German formations the British chose three of the divisions which had served with the 8th Army in the desert and in Italy to spearhead the British assault, for it was felt that their experience of battle would contribute towards a successful landing and follow-up campaign. But it was soon seen that such units did not always settle down easily to warfare in a new theatre of operations. To some extent there was a belief among the men that they had done their duty and they felt 'they were on the homeward slope and harboured an instinctive desire to enjoy a peace which, at last, seemed within the bounds of survival and possibility. . . . It would be much harder for this part of the British Army to throw itself so unselfishly into the thick of battle.'

32

Not until much later in the campaign did either 7th Armoured or 51st Highland Division regain the form which had made them famous and then only after new men had replaced those old soldiers who could not, or did not, learn to cope with the new type of fighting in north-west Europe. It was the bitter fate of 50th Division to be disbanded in November 1944, when the shortage of infantry replacements required that some divisions be broken up.

Therefore, by and large, it was the previously untested divisions which quickly adapted themselves to the peculiar nature of the fighting in Normandy. Being new to war the troops in those formations were not burdened by lessons learned in other campaigns and, therefore, were able to respond to the needs of the moment with uncluttered minds.

As we have seen the principal role of the British Army in the first weeks of the battle for Normandy was to tie down the German armour. Thus it had to bear not only the brunt of the fighting but also the criticisms and scorn of those who pointed to the more rapid advances which the Americans were then beginning to make. There was one man able to inspire the Army with his own confidence in victory and belief in itself. In some undefinable way Montgomery represented – on behalf of the inarticulate mass of his soldiers, and indeed of the working class of Great Britain – the commitment to total victory, and his understanding of their mood placed him well beyond most of his contemporaries. Montgomery's approach was, for a British General Officer, unique and almost revolutionary. His flair for showmanship stemmed in part from his realization that some sort of popular image for a military leader was an important factor in the maintenance of morale in a modern, conscript army. This could only be achieved by taking the men under his command into his confidence, by telling them exactly what he intended doing during the course of a battle and why he was doing it. It was, perhaps, less important what he said; it was the fact that he thought it important to come and talk to them, to involve them, that made them feel at long last that they were part of a team, and of a team which would liberate Europe.

As a visible sign of this sense of purpose each British Army in the field, from the early 8th Army days, had carried a shield badge as a distinction and to convey that those who wore the shields were crusaders. Indeed the emotive word Crusade was used in most of the speeches and declarations by the senior officers in their Orders of the Day and the adoption of the title 'British Liberation Army' by Dempsey's 2nd Army and by the British units serving with the Canadians was designed to foster the belief that the war which they were fighting was one of common and equal effort to free Europe.

The American Army

The events which followed D-Day tended to act as confirmation of the new balance of power which had occurred in the Allied camp and which was, eventually, to be world wide. The United States could now begin to release its carefully hoarded strength and to convert its enormous military and economic potential into concrete expressions of power. In this form of endeavour only the USSR was in a position to compete.

American fighting men had begun to land in England shortly after their country's declaration of war and to the one and three-quarter million troops stationed in the United Kingdom on the eve of the invasion of Europe, there could be little doubt that their cause was materially in the ascendant and that of their host country visibly on the decline. Inevitably there was friction between the Americans and the British servicemen, which often hinged on peripheral matters – the brashness and immodesty of the GI, and the evident lack of concern for the finer points of military etiquette. After D-Day there seems to have been a marked improvement in relationships at the lowest level of the Army which coincided with the deterioration at senior command level. Both nations, it was now felt, were shouldering equal burdens in the fight. But the basic divergencies in attitude arising out of the differences in the levels of their prosperity emerged on the battlefield where a certain degree of prodigality among US armies in the expenditure of manpower became apparent. The following comment on British combat methods, made by the historian of an American artillery unit which saw action in Italy and in north-west Europe, illustrates this.

> The British, not being as outwardly expressive as the Americans, shrugged off losses. . . . [US artillery] observers reported that they seemed callous to casualties. They sent company strength units against objectives where American commanders would have used a battalion. Later, we learned how deeply they were concerned, not only with the loss of friends but with the long-term effect of having their best manhood sacrificed in two [world] wars fought within a period of twenty years . . .

For their part British soldiers became aware that, behind their frequently brash and over-confident exteriors, the American soldiers were circumspect and modest warriors. Due to their enormous reserves of ammunition and equipment it made sense to the Americans to employ their material superiority as a matter of course in a manner which often astonished friend and foe alike.

The historian of 2nd Household Cavalry Regiment recalled an occasion when an isolated squadron of armoured cars heard reverberating through the Normandy 'bocage' at the dead of night, the sound of small-arms fire. Peering tensely into the darkness the British saw, at last,

> . . . preceded by another fusillade, the strangest of cavalcades . . . The 'enemy' were Americans . . . They were about a Company strong. In the middle of their column and sitting like Buddha on a mound of kit in the back of a jeep was an officer chewing a large cigar and studying by its glowing ash a crumpled map folded to the size of a small pocket-book. The jeep, finding it difficult to pass our vehicles and adjust its pace to the infantry, was groaning in bottom gear. Its occupant . . . casually glancing from his map to the shadowy outline of a tree, as if identifying a landmark, sprayed its topmost branches with a Tommy gun. 'Snipers', he grunted. When he ran out of ammunition, someone else took up the running; the amount of small-arms ammunition carried by these Americans must have been prodigious, for long after they had scraped by our cars we could still hear them firing at the tree tops.

The Western allies, particularly the Americans, were able to reverse the German achievements of the early war years by using their overwhelming strength in artillery, tanks and aircraft to reduce the Germans in a war of attrition, a tactic which requires no great degree of subtlety and daring. But whatever one's opinion of this tactic they nevertheless succeeded in their primary intention of defeating their enemy and also managed to keep their casualties down to an acceptable level. Their enormous material losses were therefore of little significance, but their reluctance to take what they considered unnecessary risks on the battlefield – a habit of mind also evident among the British and Canadians where the shortage of infantry replacements was a particularly acute problem towards the end of the war – cancelled out, to some degree, their material superiority. Thus the outgunned and outnumbered German soldier gained a considerable moral advantage over the Anglo-Saxons. Evidence of this can be gained from the battle report, dated 29 July, from one of the panzergrenadier regiments of 10th SS Panzer Division. 'The morale of the enemy infantry is not very high. It depends largely on artillery and air support. In case of a well placed concentration of fire from our own [German] artillery the infantry will often leave its positions and retreat hastily. Whenever the enemy is engaged with force, he usually retreats or surrenders.'

The great ability of the US Army lay in a peculiar combination of the 'frontier spirit' and mechanical ability. When the divisions of 1st and 3rd US Armies, fretful at their enforced confinement in the 'bocage' and the flooded valleys of the Cotentin peninsula, at last poured through the 7th German Army's shattered line and sped into the interior of France they demonstrated an enthusiasm for bold, reckless cavalry charges. The causes of this sudden transformation in the fortunes of Bradley's troops, whose combat performance in the 'bocage' had belied their true potential, were analysed by Chester Wilmot, who as BBC radio correspondent had witnessed much of the fighting in France. He noted:

> More than any other people the Americans are mechanically minded. . . . In their dealings with people the Americans are often unsure of themselves and betray their feeling of inferiority by their behaviour . . . but in the realm of machines they possess a sense of mastery which European peoples do not know . . . When the campaign became fluid another factor assumed almost equal importance; the survival or revival of the frontier spirit. The Americans had . . . an instinct for movement. . . . To the American troops driving across France, distance meant nothing . . . This was not the case with the majority of the British forces. . . . Dempsey had few units capable of rapid, aggressive movement. . . . By nature British commanders and men moved at a deliberate pace. In Bradley's Command . . . as soon as the breakout had been achieved, every division, armoured and infantry alike, seemed capable of swift and bold exploitation.

Thus while on the northern flank the British and Canadians fought their way forward with dogged determination against an enemy determined to hold until the very last, the Americans with their mobility were able to move faster than the Germans and succeeded in containing them within a pocket which had its origins in the abortive offensive to reach Avranches.

The Germans

'I could have made the Allies pay a fearful price for their victory.'
VON RUNDSTEDT

It will be shown in other pages of this work how German Intelligence had proved to be faulty and so shot through with inter-Service rivalries that it had been unable to forecast Allied intentions. It had been deceived as to the area, time and strength of the invasion and had even been denied meteorological data upon which to forecast the weather. Lacking this information the Wehrmacht planning staff had predicted that no invasion would come on 6 June for they based their belief that such an operation could not be launched at a time of strong winds, poor weather and choppy seas.

The poor weather of 5 June had buoyed them up and thus the first garbled accounts from the 7th and 15th Armies of massive air strikes, paratroop drops and acts of sabotage evoked expressions of disbelief on the part of the High Command.

A fundamental weakness of the German Army was that there was no unified system of command to control the deployment and employment of the one-and-a-half million men stationed in the West. There was controversy between Rommel, the GOC of Army Group 'B', and his superior as Commander in Chief in the West, von Rundstedt, and Geyr von Schweppenburg, the commander of Panzer Group West, on how the ten panzer divisions in the area of von Rundstedt's command were to be deployed.

The conflict had been brought about by the appointment of Rommel as Inspector General of Coastal Defences in Western Europe. His contention, based on personal experience, was that the panzer divisions should be deployed near the coast in order that they could deliver a counter-blow against an Allied beachhead before it had had time to consolidate. Only thereby could the effect of the Allied air assaults be negated. Rundstedt and Geyr von Schweppenburg held Rommel's proposals to be fundamentally unsound. To hold the main force close to the Channel coast would not allow time for them to be redeployed and they argued that it would be folly to commit the armoured reserves until the direction, weight and intent of the Allied operation had been firmly established. Once this was known then there could be a regrouping and a massive armoured counter-attack launched from a point well back from the coast. Their conviction was that a centrally located mobile army would be capable of driving the Allies back into the sea, whereas un-coordinated assaults by individual panzer divisions would surely fail.

Hitler settled for a compromise which satisfied neither side. Three armoured divisions, 2nd ss, 9th and 11th, would remain out of Rommel's control and form part of Army Group 'G', south of the Loire river. There they would be held to meet any of the Allied invasions of south-west France and the Mediterranean at which the London-inspired deception plans had hinted. The remainder of the armoured formations in von Rundstedt's area would be split into two. The 21st, 116th and 2nd Panzer Divisions being assigned to Army Group 'B' reserve, and 1st ss Panzer, 12th ss Panzer Lehr and 17th ss panzergrenadier Divisions in that of okw. Schweppenburg insisted on maintaining operation control over Rommel's three panzer divisions, thus interposing yet another command authority between Rommel, the Army Group Commander, and his subordinates. It must be understood, too, that the armoured forces in the okw reserve could only be committed to action with Hitler's express consent and, given the mutual contempt which Hitler and von Rundstedt had for each other's military judgement, it can be appreciated how difficult it was to be to obtain authority to move those units once the invasion had begun.

The 21st Panzer Division which was the only armoured unit near the landing beaches on the morning of 6 June was caught in an intricate web made up of rival commands. As part of Army Group 'B' panzer reserve it was released to 7th Army which then assigned it to 84th Corps, positioned in the Calvados region of Normandy. Put into the line to support 716th Infantry Division it held the British and Canadian advance inland and thus helped to limit the extent of the landings made by 6th Airborne Division east of the Orne. It might have achieved more but it was inhibited by the fact that it could not deploy completely as a panzer division. While its panzergrenadier and artillery had been sent in to support 716th Division, the panzer regiment could not be moved without the authority of Schweppenburg's Panzer Group West. Thus, 21st Panzer Division, dispersed by air attacks and confused by command decisions, was committed piecemeal. In conjunction with two severely depleted infantry divisions and without the support of the other armoured formations it had to cope with both 1st British Corps and 6th Airborne Division.

The other two panzer units which had been placed to intervene on the first day of the invasion, 12th ss and the Panzer Lehr Divisions, moved towards the beach area only after having spent most of D-Day in a state of indecision and uncertainty brought about by the refusal of okw to endorse, until late in the afternoon, von Rundstedt's decision to put them into action. D-Day was further influenced by Rommel's absence on leave, by Hitler's late rising and upon his insistence on entertaining the new Hungarian Prime Minister,

Sztojay, to the exclusion of all other business, particularly that of committing the OKW reserve to battle.

The c.-in-c. West exercised no authority over the Luftwaffe or the Kriegsmarine and this led to the most ridiculous situations arising. There had been occasions when naval shore batteries were sited without reference to and, sometimes, against Army advice and during the fighting the absurd situation arose in which targets at sea were under naval fire control, but targets engaged on the beach or during the advance inland were directed by the Army. The location of most of the anti-aircraft guns had been decided by the Luftwaffe and when, in May 1944, Rommel had called for the concentration under his command of the widely scattered batteries of 3rd Flak Corps, Reichsmarschall Goering had at first refused this obvious and sensible suggestion. Demarcation disputes such as this did not resolve themselves even after the landings had taken place and similar situations were to arise throughout the fighting, particularly in the battles within the Falaise pocket itself where units were withdrawn or put into the line without reference even to the local commanders on the ground. The more confused the situation became then that much more arbitrarily were the shrunken units moved about.

The OKW interfered with every plan and questioned every movement. It was with a certain bitter truth that von Rundstedt commented that his authority over the troops was restricted to changing the guard at the front door of his headquarters. There was, of course, a reason for this scrutiny of the activities of the field armies. On 20 July there had been a bomb planted in Hitler's East Prussian headquarters and the failure of the explosive to kill the German Chancellor as well as the inaction of the German generals privy to the plot to organize an effective revolt against the Nazi Government had resulted in wave after wave of arrests, of suicides and of executions of senior officers. After 20 July each and every one of them was suspect, and Adolf Hitler's practice as Supreme Commander of interfering with the plans and decisions of his subordinates increased.

Every position had to be held at all costs: any request to withdraw had not only to be reported but had to be accepted and agreed to before it was allowed to take place. The Führer's control was exercised down to regimental level and, on occasion, even to specifying the roads along which a particular unit was to move. Army, corps and even divisional headquarters were thus reduced to the level of clearing houses for his orders and any control over their units by senior officers could be, and frequently was, rejected by the Führer acting through the OKW.

In an atmosphere of suspicion and fear where the questioning of any order from Hitler was akin to treason it needed a commander of the strongest character which von Kluge was not. He was compromised by his association with the July bomb plotters and daily expected to be arrested. He was dragooned into the counter-attack at Mortain against his better judgement and when it failed, as he knew it must, Hitler's criticism was that 'Success only failed to come because von Kluge did not want to be successful.' When the Avranches offensive was ordered to be resumed and ss General Hausser, then commanding 7th Army, protested at the order to move a panzer division from the weak southern flank, which he saw as 'a death blow not only to 7th Army but to the entire Wehrmacht in the West', von Kluge could only reply, 'It is the Führer's order.' His resigned acceptance of the flow of contradictory orders from okw led to the death of 10,000 of his soldiers and the destruction of his army.

In the two and a half months which ran from D-Day to the last of the fighting in the Falaise pocket the German generals who strove to contain the Allied armies within the beachhead area were bitterly aware that the bravery of the men under their command was not enough to counter the material superiority of the Allies and that the orders to stand or die had condemned their soldiers to death. Nor could they be unaware that arguments for a change in the direction of the Third Reich were gaining currency; arguments whose validity in the context of the uneven struggle being conducted in the orchards, meadows and hedgerows of Normandy few of the commanders were inclined to dispute.

Their tragedy was that in von Kluge they had a man whose life and death was representative of the anti-Nazi conspiracy as a whole: decent, meandering and ineffectual.

Of the German Army in Normandy it can be said that it was typical of the state to which the whole force had been brought by the bitter years of war. Together with elite ss and paratroop units, there were other formations made up entirely, or nearly so, of aliens: prisoners of war, foreign volunteers and other low calibre troops.

The German military machine was under-equipped in the material sense. Compared to the British and us armies it was never fully mobile because the national economy, even when it could draw upon the industrial resources of occupied Europe, was unable to produce the huge numbers of motor vehicles which were needed. German industry, which was placed on a war footing only after 1942, would have been hard put to meet the increased demands in petrol which such a programme would have inevitably entailed. Thus the transport available to the Wehrmacht infantry divisions was either horse-drawn or consisted of vehicles taken from foreign or captured stocks. The procurement of artillery, armoured fighting vehicles and, indeed, many other vital items of equipment depended upon similar *ad hoc* measures. As the war progressed there were improvements both in the quantity and quality of weapons, thanks to Speer's direction of the economy and the standardizations which he introduced. But due to the antagonisms which existed within the various agencies of the Third Reich and their conflicting priorities the problems of munitions and armaments production were never adequately resolved.

A review of the fighting record of German troops in the Second World War would suggest that this material inferiority *vis à vis* the Allies did not hinder them as much as it might have a less strongly motivated army. Throughout the war they displayed an amazing capacity for improvisation; often under the most adverse tactical circumstances they were able to snatch a temporary victory from the jaws of defeat. It is, of course, true that there was a reduction in the calibre of the German infantryman and that this decline accelerated after the end of the Normandy campaign. Then underage and overage recruits were brought in, an increasing reliance was placed upon foreign volunteers and recourse was made to men who were either still convalescent or who were suffering from dietary or hearing problems.

Divisions brought from the East experienced the same difficulty in adjusting from conditions in Russia as did the Allied divisions which had come from Italy. The German units were able to overcome these difficulties by a flexibility of mind and a greater familiarity with the combat capabilities of their weapons but in the early days of the campaign their ignorance of Allied air superiority caused them losses. Some units, particularly those of the ss, had moved in daylight and rolling forward through country lanes had been caught, unable to deploy, and had been badly hit.

The Influence of Hitler

The encirclement operation which has passed into history as the battle of Falaise was, in a unique way, Hitler's folly in the west. It was a battle that under a militarily competent commander would never have taken place and it is a monument to the German Chancellor's failure in this respect and to his peculiarly rigid mental processes. Had the campaign in Normandy been conducted according to the plans and proposals of his generals then Falaise would today be an unremarkable name on the map. As it is, because the German Army was directed entirely in accordance with the Führer's will; in direct contradiction to the fundamental, tried principles of war, then it is associated for all time with a bloody battle of annihilation which marked the end of the stubborn German defence of France.

The origins of the causes which led up to the battle of Falaise go back as far as 1938, in which year, on 4 February, Hitler assumed the role of Commander in Chief of the Wehrmacht (the German Armed Forces) in addition to his title of Supreme Commander, which meant that to the title of the highest appointment in the Armed Forces the Führer of the Third Reich had added the actual direction of military operations in the field. This he chose to exercise in late 1939, when the preparations for the invasion of the West were begun. He not only told his generals *when* to attack but also *how*, leaving the Commander in Chief of the Army and his Chief of Staff with only the technical execution of the operation. As von Manstein, one of Germany's most renowned commanders in the Second World War, was to note, 'Hitler had now taken over the functions which Schlieffen believed could at best be performed in our age by a triumvirate of King, statesman and warlord. Now he had also usurped the role of warlord. But had the drop of "Samuel's anointing oil", which Schlieffen considered indispensable, really fallen on his head?' It had not and the destruction of Germany in both east and west were the bitter consequences.

It was an apposite, if bitter jest among officers that not a single soldier could be moved from a door to a window without the Führer's approval. Germany's Army became Hitler's Army, directed according to his understanding of war. As a result his failings as a military commander were reflected in the deployment of his armies in the field.

Certainly Hitler had an astonishing grasp of the purely technical characteristics of the Army. He often surprised his listeners by revealing a detailed knowledge of the characteristics of guns or tanks and by reciting the latest armament production figures, at the same time comparing them with those of months or even years previous. He may have been an able quartermaster but Hitler was no war lord. A sound strategic sense was vital, but that was totally absent.

In the years of defeat Hitler's dedication to the principle of 'no withdrawal' became an obsession. This policy had its origins in the winter battles of 1941/2, which he believed fully justified his insistence that not an inch of ground should be yielded voluntarily. Never was he to repent of this belief and until the end of the war he firmly rejected the idea of strategic manoeuvre in defence. At a conference on 10 January 1945, he declared, 'I have always had a horror when I hear that in some spot or the other we have had to disengage or withdraw in order to achieve operational freedom. For years now I have been hearing this and the result is always disastrous.' Indeed, for Hitler, the 'no withdrawal' policy was elevated from a strategic principle to a soldierly ethic, even a moral one. The adherence to the concepts of 'no surrender' and 'fight to the last man' which permeated all his orders in the last years of the war, was for him the ultimate commitment that a soldier could make to his Fatherland. Only he, the Führer, the arbiter of the nation's destiny, could make the decision whether to yield ground or not. In August 1944, a Special Issue of OKW notes for the Officer Corps, inspired by Hitler, declared, 'This decision [to surrender] is obviously for the OKW alone, and for no other . . . the word of the Führer alone can be given in explanation of the apparently senseless sacrifice involved in fighting to the last man.' Nine months later, the day before he committed suicide in the shattered ruins of his Berlin bunker, Hitler made a point of stipulating in his last Will and Political Testament, 'May it be in the future, a point of honour with German officers, as it already is in our Navy, that the surrender of a district or a town is out of the question and that, above everything else, the commanders must set a shining example, of faithful devotion to duty until death.'

It was von Manstein who made the most severe judgement on the conflict of attitudes between the Führer and his commanders when he wrote,

What weighed most heavily . . . was the perpetual struggle with the Supreme Commander to make him realise operational necessities. Our repeated demands for the establishment of maximum effort at the decisive spot . . . as well as for operational freedom of movement in general . . . were merely outward signs of the struggle. The basic issue was between two incompatible conceptions of strategy; Hitler's which arose from his personal characteristics and opinions . . . [and those] based on the traditional principles and outlook of the German General Staff. On one side we had the conceptions of a dictator who believed in the power of his will . . . [but] who fought shy of risks because of their inherent threat to his prestige and who . . . lacked the groundwork of real military ability. On the other side stood the views of the military leaders who . . . firmly believed that warfare was an art in which clarity of appreciation and boldness of decision constituted the essential elements. An art which could find success only in mobile operations because it was only in these that the superiority of German leadership and of the German fighting troops could be maintained.

Other military leaders expressed similar points of view and Heinrici recalled, 'Hitler always tried to make us fight for every metre, threatening to court-martial anyone who didn't'. Von Tippelskirch wrote bitterly, 'The root cause of Germany's defeat was the way that her forces were wasted in fruitless efforts and, above all, in pointless resistance at the wrong time and place. These were due to Hitler.'

The paralysing effect of the Supreme Commander's influence upon military operations was evident from the time of the first landings on D-Day. By 9 June it was clear that German counter-action had failed and that the Allies had firmly established themselves upon the coast of Normandy. On 9 June Rommel ordered that there should be a return to the defensive and that a planned counter-attack should be postponed until the preparations had been made and the forces for it assembled. It was on the 10th that Hitler condemned 7th Army to death when he declared, 'There can be no question of fighting a rearguard action, nor of retiring to a new line of resistance. Every man shall fight or fall where he stands.'

To this absurd policy the German commanders in the West were totally and unanimously opposed for the containment of the Allies within their lodgement area could never be permanent and the idea of a strategic withdrawal was mooted. All plans for an armoured attack were abandoned on the 11th when Schweppenburg, who had been appointed to command the panzer thrust, received intelligence that the British and Canadians were massing for a major assault on Caen. Gerd von Rundstedt knew that the German position in France was hopeless and that Germany had lost the war. He claimed, in a post-war interrogation, that had he had a free hand in the conduct of operations he would have carried out a slow retiring action exacting a heavy toll for each piece of ground given up. 'I think I could', he said, 'have made the Allies pay a fearful price for their victory.'

Rommel agreed fully with his superior and between them they drew up a new plan of campaign which would concentrate the armour for a decisive blow against the Allies. In order to achieve this they would have to withdraw from the front line the panzer divisions locked there in battle and replace the armour with infantry units drawn from the Mediterranean coast of France and from the Pas de Calais. The execution of this plan required the withdrawal of all German units behind the Orne and Loire rivers and, thereby, the abandonment without a fight of the whole of France south of the Loire. This plan was brusquely rejected by the Supreme Commander and in a conference with his two Field Commanders in the west he emphasized that there would be no withdrawal and that it was still possible to drive the Allies back into the sea. This belief was predicated upon the maintenance of the defensive ring around the Allied armies in Normandy, upon a greatly strengthened and more active Luftwaffe and upon the success of the V-weapon offensive against the United Kingdom. Not one of his three elements for victory held good.

He still considered the possibility of a counter-attack and ordered Rommel, on 20 June, to drive a corridor to Bayeux using the ss divisions which had begun to arrive on the invasion front. Rommel's task was to assault, isolate and destroy the British around Caen, but growing British strength forced him to limit the scope of the attack. While the ss embarked upon a series of local counter-attacks, von Rundstedt and Rommel were at Berchtesgaden being assured by the Führer that everything depended upon holding the line around the Allies in the lodgement area. The argument used by Hitler, according to Rommel, was that the Allies must never be given the opportunity to develop mobile warfare and that they had to be kept confined to the beachhead till they had been worn down in a war of attrition. When one considers both how heavily outnumbered was Germany on the sea, in the air and on land and the increasing potency of the Allied air offensive then Hitler's belief in the German ability to fight and to win a war of attrition can be seen to be the height of illusion. It was precisely this sort of delusion which created the conditions through which the 7th Army and the 5th Panzer Army were encircled.

Conditions deteriorated throughout the weeks leading up to the middle part of July. On the 21st of that month von Kluge, who had replaced von Rundstedt, wrote a long memorandum to Hitler and enclosed with it a report on the situation written by Field Marshal Rommel. In this memorandum von Kluge, who had come fresh to Normandy from the unreal atmosphere of the Führer's headquarters, gives an accurate account of conditions. In view of Hitler's subsequent demands for an all-out offensive, which show that he had either misread the report or misjudged its contents, the von Kluge document is quoted in full.

MOST SECRET

O.B. West   21 July 1944

My Führer,

I present to you herewith a report of *Generalfeldmarschall* Rommel which he handed over to me before his accident and which he has discussed with me.

I have now been here about a fortnight and after long discussions with the responsible commanders of the fronts here, especially those of the ss, have been convinced that the views of the *Feldmarschall* are, unfortunately, correct. My discussion yesterday with the commanders of the formations near Caen, held immediately after the recent heavy fighting, has, particularly, afforded regrettable evidence that in our present positions – including the material position – there is no way by which, in the face of the enemy air force's complete command, we can find a strategy which will counterbalance its annihilating effect without giving up the field of battle. Whole panzer units, allotted to counter-attacks, were caught in carpet bombing of such intensity that they could not escape from the torn-up ground except by prolonged effort or, in some cases, by towing them out. The result was that they arrived too late. The psychological effect of such a mass of bombs falling with all the power of an elemental force upon the fighting troops, particularly the infantry, is a factor which has to be given particularly serious consideration. It is immaterial whether such carpet bombing hits good troops or bad. They are annihilated and their material is shattered. If that occurs frequently then the power of endurance of the force is put to the severest test. In fact it stagnates and dies. That which survives is no longer a fighting force capable of meeting the situation. Consequently the force sees itself facing an irresistible power.

I came here with the fixed determination of making effective your order to hold fast at all costs. But one has to appreciate that the price which must be paid to meet that demand is the slow but sure destruction of the forces. I am thinking here of the Hitler Youth Division, which is earning the highest praise. One sees that material supplies arriving in the battle area are completely insufficient, as indeed are the numbers of personnel, and that battle needs, especially in artillery and anti-tank weapons and ammunition, are not enough to meet the demands. The result is that the brunt of the defence falls upon the ability of our brave troops and anxiety about the immediate future of this front is only too well justified.

I can report that, through the bravery of our troops and the iron will of the whole command the front has been held, although there has been an

46

almost daily loss of ground. Nevertheless, despite intense efforts the time is drawing near when this front, already overstrained, will break. Once the enemy is in open country an orderly command will be impracticable given the lack of mobility of our troops. I consider it my duty as the commander responsible for this front to bring these conclusions to your notice, my Führer, in good time. My final words at the recent commanders' conference south of Caen were, 'We shall hold out and if our situation is not improved then we shall die on the battlefield.'

Oberbefehlshaber West
von Kluge
Field Marshal

Enclosure:

MOST SECRET

Commander in Chief Army Group 'B'

Observations on the Situation

The position on the Normandy front is daily becoming more difficult and is reaching crisis proportions.

As a result of the heavy fighting, the overwhelming material superiority of our enemies, particularly in artillery and in armoured vehicles and the Allied air forces which command the battle-field without check, the losses which we have suffered have been so great that the fighting strength of our divisions is sinking very rapidly. Only a few replacements are received and due to the transport situation arrive only after weeks of travelling. We have lost about 97,000 men (of whom 2,350 were officers) . . . that is a daily wastage of between 2,500 and 3,000 men. Our material losses have also been high and have only been replaced in part, e.g. of about 225 panzers lost we have received only 17 replacements.

The infantry divisions now arriving are without combat experience, have low establishments of artillery and of anti-tank weapons. They also lack close-combat anti-tank weapons and are unable to offer determined resistance after they have been subjected to drum fire for many hours. Experience has shown that even the best units are shattered by the enemy's material superiority and by their own losses in men and material.

As a result of the disruption of the railway network the supply situation is difficult and attacks by enemy aircraft have taken place along both major and minor roads and up to 150 km behind the front line. Thus only the most essential supplies can be brought forward and artillery ammunition as well as that of mortar batteries has to be conserved. This is a situation which is unlikely to improve in the future as the enemy aircraft control the skies and are able to give the most effective close-support to their troops as a result of the construction of numbers of air-fields within the bridgehead area.

It is not possible to reinforce the Normandy front without at the same time weakening the 15th Army in the Channel coast sector, or, the Mediterranean front in southern France. But the 7th Army needs as a matter of extreme urgency two fresh divisions as its own forces have been fought to a standstill.

Masses of material and of men flow daily to the enemy and his reinforcements are not attacked by our Air Force. Enemy pressure continues to increase. Under such circumstances we must expect that within the near future, the enemy will break through our thinly held front, particularly that of 7th Army, and will thrust deep into the heart of France. I draw your attention to the attached report by 7th Army and from II Para. Corps. Except for local panzer reserves from Panzer Group West there is nothing immediately available. Marches can take place only by night because of the enemy's air superiority. There are no mobile reserves at the disposal of 7th Army to deal with a breakthrough. Our own Air Force offers little support.

The Army is fighting heroically everywhere but the unequal combat is nearing its end. It is in my opinion necessary to draw the appropriate conclusions from this situation report. I feel it my duty as Commander in Chief of the Army Group to express this clearly.

Rommel,
Generalfeldmarschall

Appendix to C.-in-C. Army Group 'B' document 'Observations on the situation'

(1) C.-in-C. of 7th Army reported verbally:
The strength of units has sunk to such an extent that some troop commanders can no longer guarantee resistance against determined and major enemy attacks. The General Officer commanding 2nd Para. Corps reports that 6,800 of 10,000 men sent as replacements have been lost. The troops lack experience and should have first been instructed behind the front line by battle-trained leaders. The present state of affairs cannot be changed unless other reinforcements are received . . .

But these warnings failed to shake Hitler. Military reality had no place in his scheme of events. July continued with the German defence being conducted on the Führer's policy of 'no withdrawal' and thus the initiative lay with the Allies. Indeed, it had done so ever since 9 June, when Rommel had ordered a temporary return to the defensive, a return which became permanent because of Hitler's intransigence. Thus the Allies were able to conduct the battle for Normandy more or less as they chose by constant attacks against and around the crucial sector of Caen. Montgomery fulfilled his strategic aim of drawing the great mass of the panzer divisions to his sector and Hitler's insistence on holding the ground kept them there and thus kept the left flank facing the Americans weak.

On 25 July the Allies exploited their initiative and the Americans began their break-out attacking the thin but fanatically defended German line at St Lô. The US thrust gathered momentum and by 31st of the month Avranches had been taken. The pronouncement of the Chief of Staff of Army Group 'B' to that piece of news was that the left flank had collapsed. Von Kluge telegraphed to Hitler: 'Whether the enemy can still be stopped at this point is questionable. Enemy air superiority is overwhelming and smothers our movements. Losses in men and equipment are abnormally high. Morale of the troops has suffered very heavily . . . infantry units consist of . . . groups which do not any longer constitute a co-ordinated force . . .'

But the Führer did nothing except exhort his commanders to hold their positions. The American break-out fanned out to Brest, Nantes, Le Mans and beyond, outflanking the southern German position. Urgent pleas for withdrawal to positions behind the Seine came to nothing. In fact instead of a retreat he ordered an attacking offensive but conceded one point, that certain of the infantry divisions held in the Pas de Calais could be transferred to Normandy.

To the Führer the break-out by 3rd US Army had given the Germans a golden opportunity to destroy the American forces. The German armour would be massed against Mortain and by a decisive thrust through the weakly held flank would smash Patton's force.

Intelligence and Deception

'Hitler believed . . . previous to and for a long time after the invasion, that a second and probably the main landing, would take place on the Channel coast.'
GEN. WARLIMONT, OKW

One of the most important intelligence coups of the war was the cracking in 1939 of the German armed forces 'Enigma' code. To confirm this insight into the intentions of the German leaders the British Intelligence services recruited an army of spies and agents in occupied Europe, whose reports, together with cross references supplied by wireless intercepts, captured documents and prisoner of war interrogations built up an almost complete and comprehensive picture of German plans, opinions and morale.

The Allied Intelligence service was thus able to devote more of its time and manpower to devising elaborate deception operations than in the more standard intelligence gathering. While it was true that the infinite cunning and subtlety of the British agencies was often compromised at junior level by careless security procedures, particularly by the Americans, the Germans, for their part, were bedevilled by the rivalry that existed between the Abwehr, the intelligence and counter-espionage service of the General Staff, and the Sicherheitsdienst, its ss counterpart. This rivalry made a rational appraisal of Allied intentions and estimates of their strength almost impossible tasks. The head of the Abwehr, Admiral Canaris, like so many of his juniors was an anti-Nazi and was determined to see that Hitler's Germany did not win the war. To ensure this the Abwehr passed to Hitler and to the OKW information that was often misleading and sometimes wildly inaccurate.

But both German agencies were themselves completely in the dark, in contrast to the British network operating throughout Europe. The Germans at no time during the Second World War had reliable intelligence coming out of Britain. The agents who were despatched by the Abwehr or the SD and who landed in the United Kingdom were quickly picked up and were either 'turned round' and sent specially doctored messages to their control in Germany, or else were tried and hanged.

Hitler's influence on the conduct of military operations has been dealt with elsewhere in this book. Here we consider how he was influenced by Allied Intelligence. The Führer had been so often right when his professional military advisers had been wrong, but after 1941 his strategic perception, although never quite dimmed, began to weaken as Germany's military situation deteriorated and his belief that his decisions were always correct was reinforced by a growing paranoia. His determination to cling to every inch of soil which his armies had won and his peculiar prognostications on the development of Allied strategy made him especially vulnerable to suggestions disseminated from London. Churchill had set up the London Controlling Section, an intelligence unit whose task it was to leak stories which hinted at major Allied operations aimed at points all over Europe. One in particular concerned Norway about which Hitler was particularly neurotic. He sent reinforcements of both Wehrmacht and ss units into that country until the occupation force numbered some 400,000 troops. This vast body of men was held, without being able to influence the course of the war in Western Europe, as a result of a Controlling Section deception plan. It is hardly surprising, therefore, that the baffled and blinded German security and intelligence agencies were of little assistance in serving their masters.

By the spring of 1944, it was clear even to German Intelligence that the scale and extent of the Allied build-up had brought the date of the invasion close and to augment its strength in the West those divisions which had suffered severe losses on the Eastern Front and which were being refitted and reinforced in north-western Europe, were not returned to Russia but were held in France and the Low Countries. In addition new divisions were raised; notably the Panzer Lehr Division, 12th ss Panzer and 17th ss Panzer Grenadier Division. At the beginning of 1944 Rommel who had taken over Army Group 'B' did much to improve the defences of the Atlantic Wall but his work was in vain for both he and his superior, Rundstedt, were deceived as to the area and time of the landings as well as the strength in which those were to take place. Allied Intelligence officers played upon the German belief that the Normandy invasion was a feint to mask the real and main Allied assault and, by deception, ensured that the German formations stationed in the Pas de Calais as well and in other threatened sectors continued to be held in position while the invasion forces landed and established a firm foothold in Europe.

In an effort to rationalize the absurd situation which had grown up out of the inter-service rivalry between the Abwehr and the SD, and exasperated by the many failures, and the undoubted treason, of many of the senior Abwehr officers, Hitler passed control of its operations to the SD in May 1944. The SD Commander, Schellenberg, entangled in the re-organisation of both services was unable to fill the intelligence vacuum in the weeks before D-Day. This resulted in a grotesque situation and one which had a direct bearing upon the location of the German forces in the West.

Hitler and the OKW calculated that the number of Allied divisions stationed in the United Kingdom was between seventy and eighty. This inflated figure was given credence by reports received from Fremde Heere West (Foreign Armies Western Section), in the Army's Intelligence evaluation department. In the months before D-Day it had been the policy of Fremde Heere West to deliberately inflate the known figures of Allied divisions in the UK, for the given figure was inevitably reduced by the sceptical but badly informed SD before they passed them on to Hitler and the OKW. This trimming of the Army figure by the SD had resulted in a reasonably accurate estimate of Allied strength being laid before the Supreme Command. But then in May 1944, the Army officer responsible for supplying the figures found himself in the acutely embarrassing and dangerous situation of having his intelligence appreciations accepted without demur by the SD because the officer who had always halved the FHW estimates had been transferred. The Army Intelligence officer could not confess to having inflated the figures to be 85 standard and 7 airborne divisions instead of the correct total of 35 divisions (including 3 airborne). Thus it appeared to Hitler that the Allies had the capacity to launch more than one invasion from Britain. This thesis was given credence by the cover plans which the Allies used as well as by the Kriegsmarine's gross over-estimate of the numbers of merchant ships which the Allies possessed.

The Anglo-Americans were well aware that Hitler and von Rundstedt believed that an invasion would be made in the Pas de Calais, a conviction based largely upon Hitler's own belief that the Allies would take steps to destroy the V.1 launching sites which were concentrated in that part of France. To meet the anticipated landing in the Pas de Calais there were eighteen divisions. Neither Hitler nor his generals could conceive that the Allies would ignore the flying bomb threat. But that is what happened for the Allied commanders took the view that south-east England would have to suffer if Overlord was to succeed. For it was preferable to have the eighteen divisions of 15th Army held where they were, protecting the V.1 sites, than have them posted to reinforce and to support 7th Army in Normandy.

The British and the Americans encouraged these false appreciations and to lend weight to the deception formed a 'ghost' Army Group – 1st US – supposedly concentrating in south-east England and preparing to invade the Pas de Calais. This phantom formation was made up of nothing more than a small headquarters staff and a large number of signallers who passed orders to and received orders from, non-existent units. This intense wireless traffic was, of course, intercepted by the Germans.

The Luftwaffe then sent reconnaissance aircraft to photograph the areas in which this phantom army was thought to be assembling and to prepare for these Luftwaffe incursions dummy vehicles, gun parks and equipment were set up and tents erected for thousands of soldiers. Vehicle tracks were made across fields, wood and canvas landing craft and embarkation 'hards' were made ready in harbours all along the coast of Kent. All these the German air force photographed to provide evidence to substantiate the details which wireless intercepts had provided.

This brilliant deception did not end with D-Day and Hitler continued to hold the great number of infantry divisions in the Calais sector. The crack panzer divisions deployed in the actual invasion area were, thus, unsupported by infantry and were drawn into battles of attrition for which they were totally unsuited. Being continually in the line they were able neither to refit nor to replace the serious losses which they suffered. Had they been available in those weeks when the Americans were accomplishing their dash to the Seine, Guderian's reproach 'Favourable chances which the boldness of the American Command occasionally offered us, we were no longer in a position to exploit', might have been reversed and there would have been no pocket at Falaise, no precipitate retreat to the Seine and no end to the war in 1945.

Terrain, Tactics and Air Power

The battlefield upon which 5th Panzer and 7th Armies were to be outflanked, confined and then destroyed can be divided into the three geological regions, the Cotentin Peninsula, the Bocage and the Coastal Plain of western Normandy. The official handbook describes them thus:

> The Cotentin peninsula can be divided into a central lowland and a northern upland. The central lowland is a cynclinal depression between the anticlines to the north and south of it. Along the east coast, the lowland includes the Carentan basin and the basin of Valognes, separated by a ridge that is continued eastward in the island of Marcouf. The plain of Carentan is flat and marshy and is liable to extensive floods. The lowland almost reaches the west coast of Cotentin, but the country here becomes more undulating in character, with isolated hills.
>
> From the central lowland the northern dissected upland rises steeply, broken only by a tributary of the Ouve. The general aspect is that of a bocage country, with dispersed settlements rather than true villages.
>
> The bocage region of western Normandy lies to the east of the basin of Rennes and rises fairly abruptly from the surrounding lowlands. A sharp edge some 150–250 m high separates it on the west from the basin of Rennes, but this edge has been considerably broken by the tributaries of the Couesnon and Vilaine. The descent to the Sarthe depression takes place in two steps, first, from the heights of the Foret d'Ecouves, the Avaloirs and the Coevrons to the plateau of Alençon, about 200 m high, and then to the incised valley of the Sarthe (136 m at Alençon and only 46 m near Le Mans). In the north there is a similar double drop to the plain of Caen.
>
> The region is highest in the north; here the two main parallel ridges, comprising the Collines de Normandie, present a considerable barrier to north–south movement. The northern ridge reaches a height of 361 m; the southern ridge reaches 346 m in the west but becomes much higher and broader eastward in the Foret d'Ecouves (417 m).
>
> The soils are, for the most part, still clays; but sandy stretches occur. The whole region, plateau and valley alike, is typical bocage country, with fields divided by hedges. The principal occupation is the rearing of cattle

and horses. The higher hills are still well wooded, but they also have large stretches of peaty swamp that become impassable in winter time.

The coastal plain of western Normandy runs east to west along a belt between Lieuvin and the Cotentin. Three main areas can be distinguished – the plains of Auge, of Caen and of Bessin. Their surface, for the most part 60–90 m above sea level, is broken only by a few north-flowing rivers; the chief of these is the Orne on which Caen stands.

The limestones of Caen have weathered into moderately rich soils favourable to wheat and sugar beet. Large open fields give a typical 'plaine' or 'campagne' appearance, in marked contrast both with the bocage country to the south and also with the adjoining clay vales of Auge and Bessin. To the west of Caen, the clay plain of Bessin is marshy, and in the lower Vire the land is reclaimed polder now devoted to dairy farming and cider production. To the east lies the Pays d'Auge, the wide alluvial valley of the Dives, with meadows and orchards stretching below the chalk edge of Lieuvin.

It was the terrain of Normandy which, to a great extent, dictated the pace of the battle and decided the tactics used by both sides. The true bocage was an intensively cultivated area of small fields and a first-class defensive country. The closed conditions helped to neutralize the Allied superiority in tanks and aircraft and thus placed the burden of the fighting upon the infantry of both sides. In each case there was a great reliance upon junior commanders for, due to the nature of the country, attacks were usually made on a very narrow frontage, usually not more than that of a platoon width. This allowed German soldiers in defence to dig positions from which they could fire their machine guns, anti-tank rocket launchers or their mortars with maximum effect, and by the use of crawl trenches withdraw themselves from Allied counter-fire and appear in a different area to open fire again.

The whole countryside in that part of Normandy was made up of little fields each enclosed within old and tall hedges set on the top of earth banks usually over a metre in height. Some of those hedges and trees along the road were so tall and their summer foliage so thick that they formed like aisles in a church, cool, green tunnels in which we could move without fear of being seen and attacked from the air.

To overcome the German defence dependent upon the thick bocage hedges the Americans fitted tanks with steel blades; thus equipped they carved passages, albeit slowly and with considerable difficulty, through the rich and almost impenetrable green barriers, so as to allow their armour to move. The American infantry, for its part, was compelled to mount an attack against each individual German position and were not happy at being involved in this slow, close-quarter, often hand to hand, fighting. Their

55

advances were only made after long drawn-out and hesitant preparations which allowed the grenadiers time to concentrate their firing power. Such was the ascendancy gained by the German infantry in the early days of the campaign that a single MG 42 opening fire could, and frequently did, pin down a whole company attack. Accustomed in training and during manoeuvres to complete and close support of armour, guns and aircraft the Americans were at a disadvantage when forced to act independently. Their infrequent patrols in the early days were badly led and carried out. Not until they had come to terms with the fact that it was a question of fighting through or dying in the bocage, did their habits change and their patrol discipline tighten to a point where they began to dominate the area and to provoke the German command into launching counter-attacks which were often driven back with heavy loss.

The verdant, heavy foliage also rendered almost impossible the task of the long-range artillery observers who could neither select visible targets nor observe the fall of shot. In such country the most important weapon was that of close support and the tanks were reduced to advancing with infantry in local and limited attacks or acting as self-propelled artillery. Experience soon showed the Germans that the long ranged and high velocity 88 mm gun fitted into the Tiger tanks was less efficient in such conditions than the 75 mm tank cannon. There was great dependency upon rocket launchers, like the panzerfaust, to destroy Allied armour and through a combination of skilful use of ground, strong nerves and the inexperience of the Americans the Grenadiers took a heavy toll.

The British area, the coastal plain from the area around Caen and extending into the Pays d'Auge, was another countryside well suited to the defence. Although more open than the bocage its copses, woods and orchards concealed the anti-tank gun line which, at long range, smashed the British tanks' thrusts, leaving the determined grenadier and his rocket launcher to destroy, at close quarters, from the cover of hedges and woodlands, the few vehicles which escaped the guns. Battles for upland areas dominated the course of the fighting and the masterly selection of ground shown by the commander of 12th SS Panzer Division, was responsible, at least in part, for the very successful defensive battle which his unit fought both before and behind Falaise.

No account of the factors which influenced the course of the fighting can be complete without acknowledging the vital, perhaps decisive, role played by the air forces. Allied air superiority was never challenged and was crushing in its effect. All German writers reveal this and admit that air power used in that way had brought a new dimension to warfare. The very numbers used against a single target were numbing. The war diary of 84th Corps reported that in one air raid no less than 1,500 bombers were used on a single battalion front.

In contrast to this shield protecting the Allied armies the part played by the Luftwaffe was insignificant and a daily average of between 250 and 300 missions were flown. These were, to a great extent, defensive in character, protecting the German rear areas or mine laying and only on one occasion was there a mass incursion of Allied air space by Luftwaffe fighters. The 84th Corps war diary reported that during the whole of June German aircraft appeared in 1/3 sector on seven occasions only.

German writers claim two reasons for the Luftwaffe's impotence at that time. Firstly, there was the British radar system through which German aircraft could be intercepted as they rose from their air-fields, and the fact that this interception was made within minutes by aircraft flying from metal link runways, laid down immediately behind the Allied front lines. This ability to know where the Luftwaffe aircraft were and to intercept them quickly drove the German Air Force from the skies.

Praise for the successes achieved by the Allied air forces is qualified by the fact that the American heavy bomber force frequently, indeed, usually caused casualties to the Allied ground forces by bombing short or even by attacking the wrong target altogether. It was mainly for this reason that bombing by heavy aircraft of targets inside the pocket was halted very early on, so that by 18 August, the bomb line could be brought no nearer to the pocket than Vimoutiers, 20 km east of the Dives.

Nothing, however, can detract from the brilliant achievements of 2nd Tactical Air Force. From the time that it struck the German panzer columns thrusting for Avranches, halted them and then destroyed von Kluge's counter-offensive within 12 hours of its opening, to the significant part it played in smashing the close-packed German columns by rocket and machine gun fire, it had an almost unblemished progress.

The few blemishes were those caused to, among others, the Polish Armoured Division when on Saturday 19 July, the congestion of aircraft above the target area led to confusion as to the identity of certain vehicle columns on the ground. Seventy-two Polish dead were the victims of this tragedy of mistaken identity. When it is considered that towards the eastern end of the pocket into an area obscured with the smoke from fires, explosions, from dust and with haze, there were moving Canadian, Polish, American, French and German vehicle columns, and that 2,000 aircraft sorties were made on that day, then perhaps, there can also be an understanding of the difficulties facing the pilots.

Thus far we have considered the factors of terrain and tactics. To conclude let us focus more closely upon the areas of the bocage and the coastal plain of Normandy. The Caen plain and the land running down to the valley of the Dives formed a vast funnel, the constricting sides of which were made up of the high ground to the south west and east and whose neck lay between Trun and Chambois. Access to those places was gained by traversing the meandering, swampy, steep-banked river Dives whose shallow waters were spanned by only a few bridges or were fordable at a limited number of crossing points. These passages across the river linked a handful of minor roads or tracks along whose narrow, unasphalted surfaces the men, beasts, arms and vehicles of the remnants of 22 German divisions were to try to make their escape, subjected day and night to artillery gun fire, to interception by tanks, and during those hours of daylight during which low level flying was possible, to the rocket and machine gunning attacks of Allied aircraft. Small wonder then that the approaches to the crossing points, the bridges themselves and the roads heading eastwards towards Gace and the Touques river, as well as the fields in all those areas were areas of the greatest bloodshed and the heaviest destruction.

This then is the scene. Pastoral peace invaded by war. A fertile countryside of high-banked, small fields in the bocage – fine defensive country – opening up to plains and to swelling downland – fair tank country – before rising into the high ground whose gradients strained alike the overworked tank engines and the weary infantry and horses as they toiled up the Mace seeking to reach Vimoutiers and safety.

Personalities

Bradley, Omar N. Lieutenant-General.

A fellow graduate of Eisenhower and of Marshall from West Point in 1915, Bradley had risen to command a division when America entered the war in 1941. During the campaign in North Africa he acted as Eisenhower's ears and eyes on the Tunisian front, and finished the campaign as commander of 2nd Corps. It was in this command that he served in Sicily and he was then chosen by Eisenhower to command 1st US Army for the Overlord campaign.

He was subordinate to Montgomery during the first two and a half months of the Normandy campaign and despite the differences in temperament between the two men they collaborated well. On 1 August 1944 Bradley was given command of the 12th Army Group which included Patton's 3rd US and Hodges' 1st Army. He was then given equal status with Montgomery who had until then been in control of Ground Troops and who still retained overall operational jurisdiction.

The standard US Army practice of allowing subordinate commanders a good deal of scope in the day-to-day running of operations and the communications difficulties which were encountered meant that Bradley's control over 3rd Army during the time of its break-out from the Cotentin peninsula was less tight than it might have been. These circumstances were, perhaps, reinforced by a reluctance on the part of Bradley to intervene in the handling of the campaign by his subordinates or his superiors.

Despite this he managed to ensure that his armies crossed the Seine – Overlord's ultimate objective – and that they were in a position to drive unchallenged through central France in pursuit of Eisenhower's strategic plan.

Dietrich, Josef. Oberstgruppenführer and Colonel General of the Waffen SS.

Born on 28 May 1892 in Hawangen, Upper Bavaria, Dietrich joined the Army in 1911 and served during the first years of the Great War with 42nd Infantry Regiment and later transferred to two first-class fighting units: 5th Assault Battalion and 13th Bavarian Tank Detachment. By the end of the Great War he had risen to the rank of Sergeant Major.

In post-war Germany Dietrich carried on the fight with the Freikorps and then turned to politics and joined the Nazi Party. He helped to form the ss Leibstandarte Adolf Hitler – the German Chancellor's own Guard Detachment – and led part of that unit in the Polish campaign and during the fighting in France during 1940. When the Leibstandarte Regiment was expanded to divisional status Dietrich led it and was also its commander during subsequent increases in strength to Corps and finally to Army status.

Among the decorations which he was awarded during the Second World War were the Knight's Cross of the Iron Cross with Oak Leaves, Swords and Diamonds.

Eberbach, H. General of Panzer Troops.

Born on 18 November 1895 in Stuttgart. Entered the Army as an Ensign during June 1914 and was posted to the 180th Infantry Regiment in February 1915. In 1920 he was transferred to the police force and returned to the Army in 1935 and rose to command 35th Panzer Regiment in November 1942. He held this command until 1941 when he took over 5th Panzer Brigade. In January 1942 he took command of 4th Panzer Division and ten months later of 48th Panzer Corps, which he led until October 1943. On 5 July 1944 he commanded 5th Panzer Army and then 7th Army on 30 August 1944 upon which day he was taken a prisoner of war.

He was awarded the Knight's Cross with Oak Leaves.

Elfeldt, Otto. Lieutenant-General.

Born in Mecklenburg during October 1895. Joined the Army as an Ensign during June 1914 and was posted to 20th Fusilier Regiment. He served in the post-war Reichswehr and by October 1935 had risen to command 2nd Battalion of 56th Artillery Regiment. Four years later he commanded the 619th Artillery Regiment and in October of that year was Chief Staff Officer of the Artillery Component of an Army Group. From 1940 to 1942 he was Chief of Staff of Artillery at Army High Command (Oberkommando des Heeres). On 26 November 1942 he took over command of 362nd Infantry Division and held that post for nearly a year when he then took over command of 47th Infantry Division. From July 1944 to August 1944 he commanded 84th Corps and was taken prisoner by the Poles when he tried to lead his group out of the Falaise pocket. He was awarded the German Cross in Gold.

Geyr von Schweppenburg, Leo. General of Panzer Troops.

Born in 1886 in Potsdam he entered the Army as an Ensign during June 1904. His first posting was to the 6th Dragoon Regiment and after the First

World War he remained in the Reichswehr. In 1933 he became Military Attaché to Brussels and the Hague and by 1937 had taken over command of 3rd Panzer Division. In February 1940 he took over command of 24th Panzer Corps and of 40th Panzer Corps some four months later before assuming command of 58th Panzer Corps in October 1942. He commanded Panzer Group West from October 1943 to July 1944 and was made Inspector of Panzer Troops during July.

He was awarded the Knight's Cross to the Iron Cross.

Kluge, Gunther von. General Field Marshal.

Born in October 1882 in Posen, von Kluge entered the Army as a Cadet and was posted with the rank of Lieutenant to the Field Artillery Regiment No. 46 in 1901. After service in the First World War and with the Reichswehr he was promoted to command 2nd Artillery Regiment during March 1930. He became Inspector of Signals Troops in 1933 and had taken over 6th Division by October 1934. He then went on to command 6th Army Corps in April 1935, No. 6 Group Command in 1938 and 4th Army during September 1939. He commanded Army Group Centre from 19 December 1941 and was then sent to be Supreme Commander in the West on 2nd July, 1944. He also commanded Army Group 'B' from 19 July to 16 August 1944.

Implicated in the bomb plot to assassinate Hitler he was recalled to Germany and committed suicide en route.

He was awarded the Knight's Cross of the Iron Cross with Oak Leaves and Swords.

Hausser, Paul. Oberstgruppenführer and Colonel General of the Waffen SS.

Paul Hausser was born on 7 October, 1880, at Brandenburg on the Havel. His first military training was as a cadet and he was then gazetted as a Lieutenant in the 155th Infantry Regiment. During the Great War he served at 6th Army Headquarters and then transferred to the Air Force.

Following service in the Reichswehr during which he rose to command a regiment, he retired from the Army in 1932 with the rank of Brevet Lieutenant General. He was then selected by Himmler to organise an ss Academy and in 1936 became Inspector General of the ss Verfügungstruppe, the forerunner of the Waffen ss.

During the Second World War he formed the 'Das Reich' Division and led it during the French campaign of 1940. He then served on the Eastern Front and was seriously wounded in October 1941. When the Allies invaded Normandy the 2nd ss Panzer Corps, which Hausser now commanded, was sent to France and he then went on to command 7th Army. During the fighting at Falaise Hausser was once again seriously wounded and lost an eye but he was brought out of the pocket. On 23 January 1945 he took over command of Army Group 'G' in the West and was taken prisoner by the Americans at the end of the war.

In addition to decorations awarded to him by the countries of the Central Powers during the Second World War he was awarded various degrees of Iron Cross, the Swords to the Knight's Cross of the Iron Cross being awarded to him on 28 August 1944.

Meyer, Kurt. Oberführer and Major-General of the Waffen SS.

Kurt Meyer, later to achieve a reputation within the German forces as 'Panzermeyer' was born in December 1910, in Jerzheim.

He joined the State Police in 1929 and five years later transferred to the 'Leibstandarte ss Adolf Hitler'. In Poland he served as a Company Commander in the motor cycle reconnaissance battalion and also fought in the Greek and Russian campaigns. By this time he had risen to command the Reconnaissance Battalion.

When it was decided to raise the 12th ss Panzer Division 'Hitler Youth', Meyer was selected to command the 25th Panzer Grenadier Regiment of the newly raised division. Upon the death in action of the divisional commander, Franz Witt, Kurt Meyer took over command of the Hitler Youth. At the age of 33 he was one of the youngest divisional commanders in the German Armed Forces.

He led his division in the fighting in the Falaise pocket and was captured at Amiens on 6 September.

For his services he received the Swords to the Knight's Cross of the Iron Cross.

Montgomery, Bernard L. General (Field Marshal from 1 September 1944).

Born in 1887 Montgomery entered the Army and served in the First World War with an infantry regiment and had a distinguished military record. By the time that the Second World War began he had risen to command 3rd Infantry Division of the British Expeditionary Forces and led it with skill during the campaign in France during 1940.

He gained a reputation as an austere and rigorous commander in several commands in the United Kingdom and was sent overseas to command 8th Army which was fighting in Egypt and Libya. He led this army to victory at El Alamein during October–November 1942 and from thence to the defeat of the Axis armies in Africa by May 1943. He led 8th Army in the campaign in Sicily and then in the fighting in Italy.

A thoroughly competent battle-field commander, a master of the set-piece battle whose main strengths were unity and clarity in command, he had his finest moments when Overlord was successfully carried through. Montgomery's relations with his American allies were often marred by misunderstandings but his dealings with Omar Bradley, his immediate us subordinate in France, were straightforward and harmonious.

Appointed to be Allied Ground Commander of all the invasion armies, as well as 21st Army Group commander, Montgomery revised an earlier invasion plan prepared by COSSAC, the predecessor of SHAEF, and laid down the strategy for the Normandy campaign which forced the Germans to concentrate the bulk of their panzer forces against the British/Canadian armies around Caen. Thereby the Americans were allowed time to accustom themselves to fighting in the cramped conditions of the bocage and to lay the foundations for that drive to the Seine during which the Falaise pocket was formed and destroyed.

Model, Walther. General Field Marshal.

Born in Genthin during January 1891, Model entered the Army as an Ensign in February 1909 and was posted to 52nd Infantry Regiment as a Lieutenant during August 1910. After service in the First World War he remained in the Reichswehr and by 1938 had become Chief of Staff to 4th Corps and by October 1939 Chief of Staff to 16th Army. He was given command of 3rd Panzer Division during November 1940 and of 31 Panzer Corps during October 1941. He then commanded 9th Army and Army Group North in January 1944, before taking over command of Army Group North Ukraine in March of that year. He was given command of Army Group 'B' during June 1944 and also took over as Supreme Commander West on 17 August 1944.

He committed suicide in 1945.

Among his decorations were the German Cross in Gold, the Knight's Cross of the Iron Cross with Oak Leaves, Swords and Diamonds.

Rommel, Erwin. General Field Marshal.

Born in Heidenheim in November, 1891 and entered the Army as an Ensign during July 1910. He was posted to 124th Infantry Regiment in 1914 and during the campaign in Italy won the Pour le Mérite. By November 1938 he was commanding officer of the Transport School and was selected to be the commandant of the Führer's headquarters during September 1939. He was given command of 7th Armoured Division in 1940 and led that formation in a victorious dash across France during the campaign in that country.

He was sent to command the German Africa Corps in February 1941 and led it through the years of its growth to Army Group Africa in March 1943. He was given command of Army Group 'B' on 1 January 1944 and was wounded shortly after D-Day. Implicated in the July bomb plot he committed suicide.

Among the many decorations he won or was awarded were the Knight's Cross of the Iron Cross with Oak Leaves, Swords and Diamonds.

Rundstedt, Gerd von. Field Marshal.

Born in Aschersleben during December 1875 Gerd von Runstedt entered the Army as a Cadet and then became an Ensign in March 1892. In June of the following year he was gazetted lieutenant in the 83rd Infantry Regiment. After service in the First World War he commanded the 18th Infantry Regiment in 1925. He then became Chief of Staff to 2nd Group Command in 1926 and was promoted to command 2nd Cavalry Division in 1928. He then took over command of 3rd Division in 1932 and Group Command No. 1 from October 1932 to 1938. He retired in that year but was recalled to service to command Army Group South for the Polish campaign. After the conclusion of that campaign he was promoted to be Supreme Commander in the East in October 1939. Following command of Army Group 'A' in the 1940 campaign he became Supreme Commander West in October, 1940.

For the Russian campaign he commanded Army Group South from June to December 1941 and was sent back to be Supreme Commander West from March 1942 to July 1944. Retired once again he was recalled, once again, to be Supreme Commander West from September 1944 to March 1945.

Among his many decorations was the Knight's Cross to the Iron Cross with Oak Leaves and Swords.

Wünsche, Max. SS Obersturmbannführer.

Max Wünsche was born in Saxony on 20 April 1914 and joined the ss Verfügungstruppe in 1934. After commissioning he took part in the Polish campaign as Hitler's ss aide-de-camp and was then posted to the Leibstandarte ss and served as commander of a motorcycle machine gun company during the 1940 fighting in France. He graduated from the ss Military Academy and took over command of the Leibstandarte's Panzer Regiment.

He was then posted to the 12th ss Panzer Division 'Hitler Youth' and was given the task of setting up the divisional panzer regiment which he then led into action in the Caen area during June 1944. In the Falaise pocket Wünsche was wounded and taken prisoner.

He was captured before he could be awarded the Swords to the Knight's Cross of the Iron Cross.

2

INTO BATTLE

The Western Flank

'The left flank has collapsed.'
CHIEF OF STAFF, ARMY GROUP B TO VON KLUGE, 31 July 1944

During the last weeks of July 1944, the Allies, although still contained within a lodgement area of Normandy, had managed to expand their bridgehead and by this steady progress, together with a build-up of men and materials, arrived at that stage in their operational plan when a break-out from the confines of the beachhead could be undertaken.

The Allied line ran from a point east of Caen and extended in a general south-westerly direction to the west coast of the Cotentin peninsula. Around Caen was situated 1st Canadian Army and on its right 2nd British Army, these two constituting 21st Army Group. On the right of Dempsey's 2nd Army was the 12th US Army Group with 1st US Army in the line and 3rd US Army, which would not become operational until 1 August, preparing itself for a mobile and active role in the forthcoming battles.

Containing these Allied armies were the divisions of Panzer Group West, originally commanded by Geyr von Schweppenburg and later during the fighting to pass under the control of Eberbach. Panzer Group West faced the Canadians and British. Deeper into Normandy was Dollmann's 7th Army opposing the British right wing and the 1st US Army.

Time was against the German command. Each shipload of fresh Allied troops or squadron of tanks debarked in Normandy made their defeat the more certain and against this massive Allied build-up they could expect to receive only the absolute minimum of men and supplies to maintain a battle line which was too long for the numbers available. Losses exceeded replacements. By the end of July the German Army in Normandy had lost 127,347 men and had received only 14,594 as replacements. During the same period 250 tanks had been destroyed and only 17 machines sent forward to fill the gap. Hitler's intention, as expressed to von Rundstedt and to Rommel, the two senior German commanders in the West, was to fight a war of attrition; to wear down the Allies and so weaken them that they could be driven back.

Von Kluge, who then replaced von Rundstedt as c.-in-c. West, forecast in a letter to Hitler, dated 21 July, '. . . that the moment has drawn near when this front, already so heavily strained, will break . . .', and his restrained comments were reinforced by Rommel's more emotional statements, '. . . on the enemy's side new forces and masses of war material are flowing to

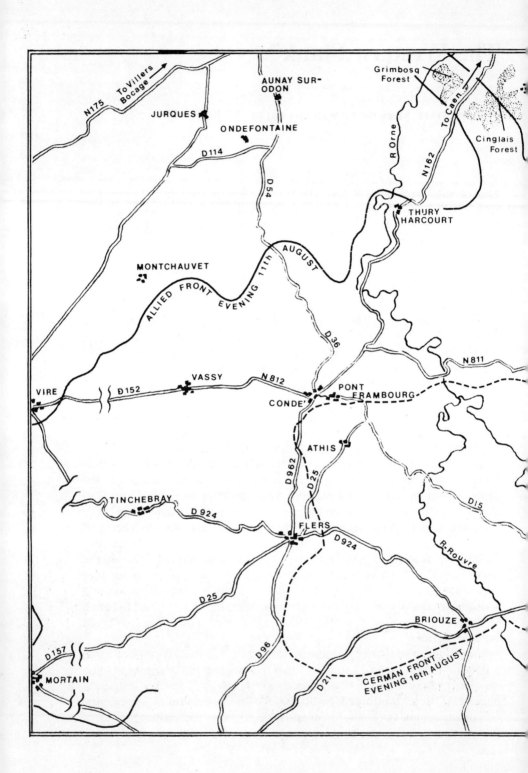

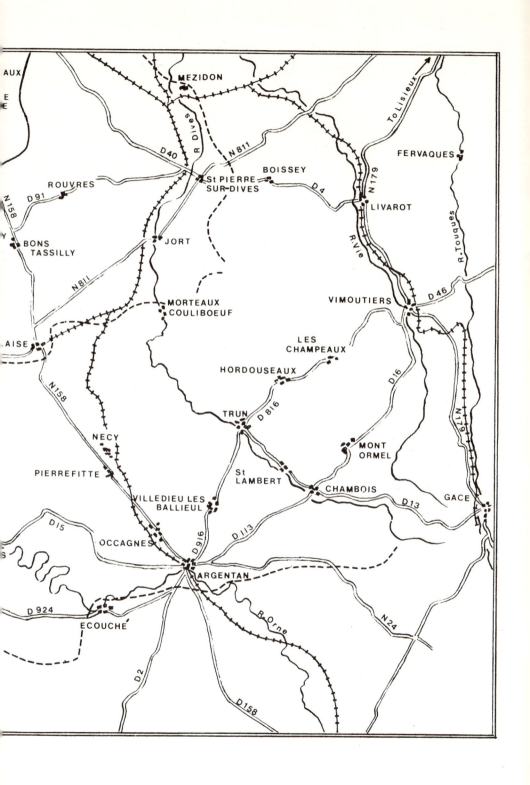

the front . . . no mobile reserves to defend against . . . a break through are at the disposal of 7th Army. The force is fighting heroically everywhere but the unequal combat is nearing its end. It is, in my opinion, necessary to draw the appropriate conclusions from this situation.'

The appropriate conclusions to which Rommel referred were to accept and to act upon Rundstedt's plan for a major withdrawal. Aware that the weak German forces could not keep the Allies close-confined in the bridgehead indefinitely and aware that his forces could not fight a successful, mobile armoured campaign von Rundstedt proposed to take Army Group 'G' out of southern France and to locate it on a temporary line running from Paris to the Swiss frontier. With this accomplished he foresaw a withdrawal by all the German forces in the West to a firm and permanent line along the West Wall (Siegfried Line) and the Rhine. Such a course of action was totally unacceptable to Hitler who insisted on no withdrawal at any point and ordered that the main weight of the German effort in Normandy be moved from between the Orne and the Vire – the centre of the German line – to the eastern flank around Caen, the retention of which area he saw as vital to his plans.

This course of action weakened the German left wing and the concentration of the bulk of the panzer forces on the Caen sector showed that they were reacting exactly as Montgomery had forecast. To hold the Caen sector to the last was the order which was responsible for the hard and bitter fighting which occurred along the northern and eastern walls of the pocket, in contrast to the less violent fighting on the southern flank. The German commanders had little idea of the power of the 3rd us Army until it was too late. It was not that the German units holding the line from Domfront to the Loire at Angers fought less bravely or with less determination, but that there were fewer of them to resist the American thrusts – at one time a single panzer division, one infantry division and a few security battalions. Even this small force was reduced when the panzer division was posted northwards to take part in an offensive around Mortain.

Between Caen and Cotentin there had been, was, and would be, much bitter fighting, for this was the area in which élite units of the German Army were located: 1st ss Panzer Division, 10th ss Panzer, 21st Panzer and II Para. Corps. But it is not with those formations that this first account deals but with a standard Army Corps, the 84th, whose position was at the left of the German line touching the sea in the Cotentin peninsula. It was in the sector held by 84th Corps that the American break-out began and it was that Corps which held the western end of the pocket which was formed, was the strong support of 47th Panzer Corps during the Mortain offensive and which conducted itself with remarkable efficiency throughout the fighting withdrawal out of the pocket.

We then begin the account of the western wall of the pocket during the last days of July 1944, shortly after American troops in an operation code-named 'Cobra', launched a week after the capture of St Lô, had ruptured the front of 84th Corps in a battle to the south and to the south-east of Coutances.

The general situation in which 84th Corps was placed on the morning of 30 July was one with which it was to grow bitterly familiar in succeeding weeks. Its front had been broken and American penetrations had separated it from its right flank neighbour. In desperation, Elfeldt, the Corps Commander, wirelessed to 7th Army. The mass of his command lay between Percy and Gavray, behind the protection of the Sienne river, while his left-wing division, 91st L L, held the line from Gavray to the coast. To defend this 20 km length of front he had 243rd Division, now reduced to a strength of just over 200 men, the remnants of 275th Division numbering less than a battalion and the fragments of 353rd Division, together with the weak and shattered 91st L L Division.

Throughout 30 and 31 July American penetrations of Corps front confirmed Elfeldt's fears that the outpost line along the Sienne would be driven in and that further thrusts by the US armour would prise loose from the sea flank the tenuous hold of his battered command. To support him 7th Army at last acted and sent forward a battle group made up of sub-units from 17th SS Panzer Grenadier Division and from 2nd SS Panzer Division, with orders to block the Avranches road. This move came too late to prevent the left wing from crumbling and was too weak to drive back the American armour. A Combat Command of the US Army struck the Engineer battalion of 5th Para. Division holding position at Le Repos, south of Carences, flung it aside and drove on towards Avranches riding down the exhausted and defeated survivors of 91st L L Division. This shattered remnant had no hope of resisting the flood which now poured down upon it and in an effort to evade it, withdrew towards Granville only to find that the town had already fallen. The German left wing no longer touched the sea – the battle line had been cracked wide open. Ahead of the US tanks there were now only disordered groups and only lack of confidence on the part of the US tank crews, unable to comprehend that they had broken out of the confines of the bocage, held them back from a rapid exploitation of the success which they had gained. The tragic situation which then developed can be claimed to have begun as the result of a mistake in direction. Seventh Army authorised 84th Corps to withdraw but not in a south-westerly direction in the direction of Rennes but south-easterly to gain touch with the remainder of the Army. Acting upon these instructions Corps swung its left wing back from the sea thereby creating a breach, albeit small, which was to be exploited by the American armour and which was to threaten with being rolled up the southern wing of the German Army in Normandy.

Corps avoided immediate encirclement during the night of 30/31 July, by withdrawing to the line Percy–Villedieu–Avranches but Army disclosed no plan to close the open left wing. Elfeldt regrouped his forces and formed them into two battle groups. The newly arrived 116th Panzer Division had added to it the surviving units of the 91st L L and 243rd Divisions and this group held a front from L'Epine to La Sée. The second battle group was made up of 5th Para. and elements of 275th Division holding the left flank and also given the task of blocking the roads eastwards from Avranches, but both to the east and to the south of this battle group there was a yawning gap.

Cautious American armoured probes revealed the weakness of the German force and these probes then became attacks which grew in strength and frequency throughout the whole of 31 July, unleashing against the thin line of German grenadiers and armour a hurricane of fire supported and supplemented by aerial attacks carried out by fighter/bomber and heavy bomber forces. Under this terrible pressure the Corps front began to give and the sector on either side of Villedieu, held by 353rd Division, was the first to crumble. To reinforce it a Grenadier regiment from 363rd Division was rushed up but the defence was still too weak to hold the American attack which drove a deep salient and threatened with encirclement the battle group of 116th Panzer Division. While Corps struggled with this crisis another attack in the Brécey region ruptured the line afresh and, as if to crown this series of setbacks, Avranches fell that day. In a despairing effort to restore the front the main force of 116th Panzer Division was put into a counter-attack and advanced with such *élan* that by last light a weak but continuous line had been reformed.

On the morning of 1 August, 1944 listeners to German radio stations heard the OKW communiqué announce a deterioration in the military situation in Normandy, that the fighting was now no longer restricted only to the lodgement area and to the Cotentin peninsula, but also the US forces there had begun a wide enveloping sweep. From a map it was clear that should this eastward swing succeed the German position in Normandy was untenable and, more seriously still, that unless there were sufficient strong forces to hand the German Army might be compelled to void the whole of northern France without a struggle.

Alarmed by the black news from Army Group 'B' that the left flank had collapsed von Kluge sent an appreciation of the situation to Hitler which included the following sentences, '. . . whether the enemy can still be stopped at this point is questionable . . . losses in men and equipment are extraordinary. The morale of the troops has suffered very heavily under constant, murderous enemy fire, especially since all infantry units consist only of haphazard groups which do not form a strongly co-ordinated force . . .' In stating this view von Kluge, who had succeeded von Rundstedt only weeks previously, was repeating the conclusions for which his predecessor had been replaced. He had come to France from Hitler's headquarters determined to carry out his Führer's orders but his subordinates had quickly proved to him that the military situation in Normandy was not that which it was believed to be at OKW. Army Group 'B', in particular, whose officers had accurately forecast the point at which the American break-out would occur, had also shown that the forces under their command were too weak to halt this and that they were powerless to prevent the US troops from bursting into the heartlands of France. The very best that they and their understrength armies could do would be to delay the event.

It would have been uncharacteristic of von Kluge to have ignored the gap on the left wing and his plan to close it was in line with the OKW directive which ordered him to hold the Caen–Avranches line. Even as the American tank men began their forward movement, von Kluge arrived at 7th Army HQ in Mortain, filled with determination to launch the counter-attack which would close the gap. The staff officers of 7th Army emphasized that the success of the operation would depend principally upon the number and flow of reinforcements, firstly to launch and then to maintain the impetus of the offensive. The usual search was made for troops who could be made available. The 84th Division which had come under 84th Corps command was posted to the Sourdeval area with orders to take over from 116th Panzer Division and thereby free it for its role in Operation Liège, the offensive to close the breach in the German line.

The intention of this offensive, as von Kluge and his subordinates saw it, was both local and tactical: to reseal the American forces within the Cotentin peninsula by breaching the gap at Avranches. This would necessitate a withdrawal of forces from less sensitive sectors of the front with a consequent temporary weakening of those areas and would create the risk that the Allies might exploit this weakness. However, while discussions at 7th Army were still in progress General Warlimont arrived from OKW bearing with him Adolf Hitler's personal plan for the attack. This was to be no short-term rebottling of the Americans within the peninsula. Here was a glorious opportunity for a strategic counter-blow which would strike into their flank and rear and cut off 3rd US Army's tank spearheads from their supply depots and reserves. The intention was not only to reseal the Cotentin but to thrust northwards, to drive the Americans into the sea and, thereby, to bring about a total collapse of the Allied front in Normandy.

Hitler's plan was simple in design, fixed and rigid in its construction. The details were, as usual, precise, but were totally unreal and were predicated upon false premises. In a letter which von Kluge wrote shortly before his suicide he referred to Operation Liège. 'Your orders were based upon conditions which did not exist. When I read your orders I had the feeling that what was being demanded of us was something which history would register as a wide-ranging operation of the greatest daring, but one which was, unfortunately, incapable of realization in practice.'

73

All preparations required to launch even a simple attack are time consuming and those movements involving the drawing off of units from other sectors, and which would be essential to the success of Operation Liège, were so protracted that nearly a week was to pass before the counter-attack could be launched – and each day's postponement worked to the advantage of the Allies.

The commanders and staff officers of both 7th Army and Panzer Group West – soon to be retitled 5th Panzer Army – raised objections to Hitler's plan for, they argued, the withdrawal of strong armoured forces from the Caen area, which was fundamental to the success of the operation, would leave that sector dangerously weak and almost defenceless against future British offensives. For their part the officers of 84th Corps were alarmed at the burdens which their severely weakened formation would have to bear in the offensive. Each of its tasks was vital. Before the opening of the assault it would have to protect the concentration area by maintaining the front against American pressure, and during the offensive its understrength divisions would have the task of protecting the right wing of the assault. Both these exacting tasks were being demanded of a formation whose numbers grew fewer with each American attack and to which only a minimum of human and material replacement was being sent. As an example of this the 84th Division which had but recently arrived was made up of men without any combat experience and could be rated only as of very low fighting quality.

The strong American pressure continued against Corps throughout 2 August and attacks came in along a front which extended from the western edge of the Severs forest, where 353rd Division held post, to Brécey, on the left wing, which was lost during that day. Although the counter-attacks by 116th Panzer Division prevented a complete break-through it was so heavily engaged in the fighting around St Pois that its relief by 84th Division could not be carried out. The reconnaissance battalion was, in fact, the only unit to be taken out of the line. The onset of darkness brought only slight relief but with first light pressure was once again applied in 116th Division's sector, to the west of St Pois. There could now be no question of relieving that division for not only was it held fast in battle but 84th Division had had its relief orders countermanded and was retained in the Sourdeval sector to hold the forming-up area against threats to the southern wing. To help seal off the break-through which threatened on 116th Panzer Division's front a battalion of self-propelled guns was brought out of Army's scanty reserve and placed under Corps command.

Fighting flared south of Sée, an area in which there had been until that time only vigorous American reconnaissance and 275th Division was struck, recoiled and fragmented under the repeated, heavy blows of the us tank men. The armoured fists of the 3rd us Army struck across the

Avranches–Mortain road, seized Juvigny-le-Tertre and careered onward until by evening they had attained the heights north of Mortain, from which they would have descended to continue their headlong advance had not a hastily assembled and hard-fighting outpost line from 84th Division first slowed and then halted them, just outside the small town of St Barthélémy.

The reconnaissance battalion of Panzer Lehr Division flung out small detachments between Mortain and Passais, thus ensuring that there was at least a thin screen along Corps' southern flank. During 4 August there was a withdrawal to a shorter line which allowed 116th Panzer Division to be taken, at last out of the line. Fresh penetrations in the Sever forest and around Le Mesnil-Gilbert brought new crises and the fear grew that Corps might find it impossible to maintain its positions against the American assaults and thus fail to carry out its part in the preparations leading up to the great counter-offensive.

By 5 August Army was nearly ready to open the operation. For the thrust towards Avranches it had been allotted 120 of the 700 tanks still in action, from the total of 1,400 which had been in service on D-Day. The plan for the Mortain offensive was that this armour would cross the ground between the Sée and the Sélune rivers, using those water courses to protect the flanks of the advance and along roads which, in the attack area, ran on east-west axes, that is to say towards and away from the Americans, thus not only facilitating the advance towards the objective but also allowing a smooth forward flow of reinforcements.

The preparations for Operation Liège led to a reshuffle of the troops on 84th Corps front and all units south of La Sée, including 116th Panzer Division, were posted to 47th Panzer Corps, the spearhead unit of the attack. During 5 August near Vire the 363rd Division was so badly hit by British attacks launched by 8th Corps, that a battalion of infantry and assault guns had to be sent forward to restore the line. In a hard little battle the British, whose sector this had now become, lost ten tanks. At Champs du Boult a fresh penetration threatened to breach the line but the hard-hit 353rd Division rallied, counter-attacked and wiped out the salient but, as if to counter balance this defensive success, the untried and weak 84th Division was driven back to Perriers-en-Beaufical in such disorder that only a hastily formed battle group of 116th Panzer could seal off the area.

During the next day the Allies gained still more ground as a result of fresh and heavy attacks. The de la Haye forest and the Champs du Boult were both wrested from their German defenders and Allied forces advanced as far as Gathémo but were then held west of Vire and at Point 119, a hill of local strategic importance to the south-west of the town. But these victories were not cheaply bought and twenty-eight of the Allied tanks were destroyed and scattered across the battle-field.

While on the German side plans had been formulated which would

75

contain the Allies, Montgomery, Commander of the Allied Ground Forces, had issued an order whose execution was to end with the destruction of the two German armies in Normandy. The plan was designed 'to destroy the enemy forces west of the Seine and north of the Loire rivers'. By opening Operation Liège, the German armies were to put their head into a sack and the farther west that they advanced the greater the certainty of their utter ruin.

It was Sunday the 6th of August and so far as it had been possible to make them so the battle plans for Operation Liège were complete, although it was appreciated that there had been too little time to perfect all the time-tables. Hitler had wanted the offensive to be held back until the strong forces essential to its success had been gathered, but to von Kluge, deeply concerned at the growing momentum of the American drive on the southern wing, each hour lost produced a fresh crisis. The attack had to be made at the latest on 7 August and now all along the German front they waited upon the arrival into the concentration area of the units called from the other sectors.

Detachments from 2nd Panzer Division drove in late in the night of 6 August and during the early hours of the following morning were followed by other parts of the Division and from the other formations chosen to form the strike force. A panzer battalion from 1st ss Panzer Division 'Leibstandarte ss Adolf Hitler' had been withdrawn from the British front on 3 August and ordered to drive with best possible speed to the concentration area. In carrying out this injunction the battalion had to travel by daylight and was attacked by Allied aircraft to such effect that the wastage rate during the drive rose to an alarming thirty per cent. One Leibstandarte officer wrote of that drive, 'we have had no experience of fighter/bomber attacks on this scale', and so severe were the delays that the Leibstandarte was still miles short of the start line when the first attacks went in.

Zero hour for the troops of the pincer arm striking to seize St Abbaye Blanche was at midnight on 6/7 August, and the first detachments set off into a dark night made more obscure by a damp thick mist. Shortly before dawn the roar of tank engines announced that the armoured spearhead was about to move off and at first light the panzer squadrons swung out of concealment, shook down into tactical formation and roared in the direction of Avranches some 40 km distant. The attack commanders were jubilant. Hitler had promised that bad weather would stop all attacks by the Allied air forces and his promise had been kept for mist shrouded and hid the panzer columns from Allied air observation. Perhaps his second prophecy might also be realized; that the Americans would not fight.

Compact, battle hardened and confident the columns of 47th Panzer Corps drove forward. The armoured wedge of part of 116th Panzer Division would advance along the valley of the Sée and strike for Avranches while

2nd Panzer Division, reinforced by the 'Leibstandarte' battalion and elements from 2nd ss Panzer Division, swung round on either side of Mortain. This first wave would be followed by a second made up of detachments from 17th ss Panzer Grenadier Division and from the Panzer Lehr Division.

The first bound gained eight km and was everywhere successful. Mortain was recaptured and part of 117th us Infantry Regiment (30th us Division) which had been defending St Barthélémey was overrun and driven from the town in disorder. As the morning and the panzers both advanced the hot sun began to disperse the mist and Allied aircraft swooped low over the tank columns strung out along the road and bombed them into immobility. The attack by 2nd Panzer Division had failed to take Juvigny and the 'Leibstandarte' battalion, now less than a company strong, was ordered to revive the attack and to bring it forward. As the ss vehicles advanced there swept down upon them wave after wave of aircraft from the RAF's 2nd Tactical Air Force and from 9th us Air Force and Allied mastery of the air brought about the first example of an armoured assault being halted by air attack alone.

Then as the baffled armour roared around the fields seeking to avoid the rockets which were poured out upon them the American 7th Corps began the first counter-offensives, its troops coming in with a rush and supported by aircraft. Under this double blow the 47th Panzer Corps staggered, halted and was pushed back to its start line. While on the Mortain front the panzers had been conducting an offensive, on 84th Corps sector there had been bitter defensive fighting. Barely had the first troops of 47th Panzer Corps moved out into the assault than the 29th us Division smashed forward and captured Vire, sustaining in their attack enormous losses. Such was the power of this thrust and so many were the penetrations of Corps front that cooks, batmen and drivers had to be formed into rifle platoons and sent post haste up the line. During that day Ondefontaine fell to the British 43rd Division and assaults were opened upon Montpinçon, a hill of great strategic importance south west of Caen.

With the failure of the Mortain offensive fresh and heavy blows were rained down upon 84th Corps driving it back to a line south east of Vire and extending to Perriers. Even this withdrawal was insufficient to shake the persistent Allies and 363rd Division was badly mauled. To Corps' plea for help 7th Army could offer nothing but advice to restore the situation by counter-attack, for preparations were going ahead to renew the offensive to capture Avranches. Hitler, encouraged by the defensive successes which had been gained in the fighting on the Canadian front around Falaise, had decided to strike once again to achieve his strategic dream in the Cotentin peninsula.

Corps gathered its forces for a counter-attack. Two recently arrived battalions from one of 331st Division's regiments were concentrated together with a battalion from 84th Division, one armoured battle group from the Panzer Lehr Division and another made up of the remnants of 1st ss Panzer Division's battalion. When the attack opened during the night of 9/10 August the first advances drove back the Americans from the positions which they had reached. The pincer arm mounted by 363rd Division gained the Maisoncelles–Jourdan cross-roads while 353rd Division reached St Germain-la-Talavende but then us ripostes drove back the German troops. Throughout that night and the following day the fighting swayed back and forth as the Americans strove to break through to the south east of Gathemo and 84th Corps sought to hold them. Bitter tank and infantry fighting ensued and the losses sustained reduced even further the strength of the shattered battalions until Corps was too weak to clear up any further penetrations of its front and battle groups from the 'Leibstandarte' and 116th Panzer Division had to be committed. The 84th Corps, like the rest of the German forces in Normandy, was bleeding to death.

While Corps was conducting its fighting withdrawal a significant change of emphasis had occurred at the highest level of command. Von Kluge was deeply concerned at the threat posed by the 15th us Corps in its strike towards Alençon as well as by the downward drive by the Canadians. But brilliant defensive battles on the road to Falaise had held the advance and this left von Kluge free to turn his full attention to the threat on the southern flank.

What was needed were strong panzer formations to be detached from the western flank, around Mortain, and the need was pressing. Von Kluge was wise enough not to ask Hitler directly for permission to withdraw the forces from the Mortain area but merely asked that the panzer divisions 'be temporarily transferred from the Mortain area . . . to destroy enemy spearheads thrusting northwards . . . to render possible the prosecution of the decisive offensive (that is the attack towards Avranches)'. Hitler treated this application with the gravest suspicion and made no decision until 11 August. Although he had been forced, reluctantly, to authorize this switch of armour to Alençon he still demanded that the Avranches offensive be borne in mind, for he still considered possible this assault to the sea. General Warlimont wrote of this obsession: 'this was a completely unrealistic objective, but the Supreme Commander clung to it, issuing a bewildering series of orders, each following the other with ever-increasing rapidity and, with equal rapidity, being overtaken by the ever faster-moving course of events . . .'

For the German 7th Army 9 August had been a critical day. To the north the new Canadian offensive had opened with heavy bombing covering and supporting a massive armoured blow while on the deep southern flank the 3rd us Army had reached Le Mans and had begun its drive from that town.

By the evening of 11 August it was clear that the German intention to attack once again towards Avranches was unrealizable, at least so long as the situation on the southern front remained unresolved. During the night of 11 August Hausser, the Army Commander, considered the practicability of launching Panzer Group Eberbach in a counter-attack against the left flank of 15th US Corps, but other sectors produced even greater priorities. While 15th Corps had been swinging in its vast left wheel two other Corps of 1st American Army, 7th and 19th Corps, had been given the task of reducing and then destroying the salient west of Flers while 5th US Corps struck southwards from Vire. At the same time Dempsey's 2nd Army was pushing forward from the north west in conjunction with the Canadian drive from the north. Thus the Germans west of the Orne were being constricted and were to be crushed against a ring of Allied troops, the last link of whose ring of steel would be cast from Argentan to Falaise.

The 84th German Corps had a disastrous night on 11 August. Although a withdrawal had been authorized this had been limited to only 2 km and during the withdrawal units of the corps had been overtaken by the closely pursuing Americans. Then Corps established that the divisions on its flanks had not limited their withdrawal to 2 km but had moved back farther and faster leaving it at the point of a salient and under constant, heavy attack from three sides. Similar limited withdrawals during succeeding nights led to the same sort of confusion when US units struck the right-wing boundary between 84th Corps and II Para. Corps. Neither unit had the strength to deal with this incursion and each blamed the other for the fact that it had happened and that it had not been cleared.

Before the great battles in the pocket are dealt with in detail let us locate the German units holding the lines as at 11 August; that is shortly before the withdrawal began from the Mortain pocket.

On the western and southern walls of the pocket there was 7th Army with its tactical headquarters at St André. Under its command was II Para. Corps made up of 3rd Para. Division and a battle group from Panzer Lehr Division holding a front from Chênedollé to Vire. The 84th Corps contained 363rd Division, parts of 353rd Division's battle group, the 331st and 84th Infantry Divisions and 116th Panzer Division. The Corps front extended along a line from St Germain to Sourdeval. The 47th Panzer Corps, with 2nd Panzer Division and elements of 1st and 2nd SS Panzer Divisions, was concentrated around Sourdeval and Mortain. The 58th Panzer Corps with a battle group from 17th SS Panzergrenadier Division, the 9th and 10th SS Panzer Divisions held the northern edge of the Mortain woods and the ground up to Domfront. The 81st Corps which had under command elements of 708th Division, parts of 5th Para., 9th Panzer and companies of 1st Security Regiment, held a line from Domfront to Fresnay.

The 5th Panzer Army on the northern front had its headquarters at

Meulles. The 86th Corps with 711th, 346th, 272nd Infantry Divisions and the 16th GAF Division held a line from the coast via Troarn to St Sylvain. On its left flank was I ss Panzer Corps, made up of a battle group from 89th Division, 12th ss Panzer Division and 343rd Infantry Division covering a front from St Sylvain to Thury-Harcourt. The 74th Corps with 277th, 276th, 326th Divisions as well as a battle group from 21st Panzer Division under command, held the ground from Thury-Harcourt via the Druance river valley to Estry.

By Saturday 12 August, the withdrawal or the reshuffle of the forces, and to which Hitler had so reluctantly given his consent on the 11th, was in full swing. Hard on the heels of the withdrawing 47th Panzer Corps came the Americans who went on to recapture Mortain. British 12th Corps had gained touch with Canadian 2nd Corps south of Caen and Allied pressure applied along the whole of the battle line achieved great gains at some places and advances of only limited extent at others.

As if to underline the warnings which he had been sending, von Kluge forwarded to Hitler on 14 August his weekly situation report in which he stated that 'the enemy's first main objective . . . is to outflank and to encircle the bulk of 5th Panzer Army and 7th Army on both sides', and when, two days later, there had been no reaction from the Supreme Commander von Kluge decided on his own initiative to bring out the remnants of 2nd ss Panzer Corps and ordered Hausser to withdraw from the pocket the soft-skin vehicles and the train of his corps. Similar carefully hinted-at instructions went out to other commanders with the intention of removing as quickly as possible from the road to the east and thus out of the pocket, the slow moving, vulnerable and numerous horse-drawn waggons in order that when the time came for the armour to make its move back the roads might be free of traffic.

Kluge had gained a partial victory and issued orders to withdraw from the Mortain salient, this shortening of the front allowing a small reserve to be assembled which would carry out the counter-attack against the Americans on the southern wing. The build-up and the course of this offensive will be described in following sections of this book.

The 15th of August was a black day for Hitler. The Allies invaded southern France and von Kluge, caught in a bombing raid and then in a monster traffic jam, was so long absent from his headquarters that he was suspected by his Supreme Commander of plotting treason with the Allies. For the troops in the pocket the 15th had also been a black day. The American capture of St Saveur de Chalieu and St Christophe de Chalieu produced a crisis of unparalleled severity and to close the breaches in the line men were taken from any available sources. One group which was rushed up the line was a unit from Norway that had been heading for Germany to go on leave. This group was intercepted and pushed into the

1. The Allied commanders for 'Operation Overlord'. From left to right Lieut. General C. Hodges, Lieut. General H. Crerar, General Sir Bernard L. Montgomery, Lieut. General Omar Bradley and Lieut. General Sir Miles Dempsey. (*Impérial War Museum*).

2. Lieut. General Omar Bradley and Lieut. General Gerow.

3. Field Marshal Gerd von Rundstedt.

4. Field Marshal Gunther von Kluge.

5. Field Marshal Walther Model.

6. Obergruppenführer Paul Hausser.

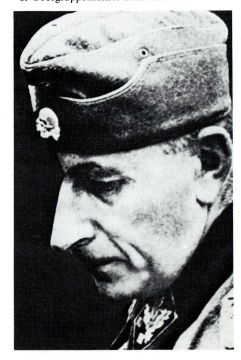

7. Field Marshal Erwin Rommel.

8. Oberführer Kurt Meyer, GOC 12th SS Panzer Division.

9. Obersturmbannführer Max Wünsche.

10. Field Marshal Gunther von Kluge in a battlefield conference in Normandy.

11. General der Panzertruppen Geyr von Schweppenburg.

12. LEFT Oberstgruppenführer Josef 'Sepp' Dietrich.

14. RIGHT Self Propelled artillery of the 1st SS Panzer Division (LSSAH).

13. ABOVE Shermans of 13/18th Hussars in the bocage shortly after D-Day.

15. A Panther and a group of panzer-grenadiers crash through a bocage hedge in Normandy.

16. Panzer V, the Panther, in action.

17. An SdKfz 7/1, 8 ton half-track, mounting a 2cm flak. Typical of the light anti-aircraft guns with which the Germans tried to defend their columns against the Allied fighter/bombers.

18. A 3.7cm anti-aircraft gun on an SdKfz 6/2 half-track mounting, here being demonstrated to children (probably not Normandy).

19. German flak troops in training. This is a 2cm flak 30, mounted on an SdKfz 10/4 and capable of use also as an anti-tank weapon.

20. FACING PAGE SS panzergrenadiers of a battle group assembling to mount an attack.

21. A company headquarters of an SS panzer-grenadier unit waiting for orders to open an attack.

22. Men of an 81mm mortar team.

23. ABOVE In addition to the anti-tank guns the German anti-tank weapons included rocket launchers such as this Panzerschreck.

24. The strain of battle shows in the faces of these SS Grenadiers. The case slung on the back of the nearer man carried the spare barrel for the machine gun.

26. RIGHT A 7.5cm pak camouflaged in a Normandy corn field.

25. A machine gun team of Waffen-SS Grenadiers on the Normandy front. The weapon is the fast firing MG 42, here used in an LMG role.

27 & 28. FACING PAGE Two aspects of the fighting in Normandy; the confidence of the Allied advance under an air umbrella and German transport with warning signs along the road warning of low flying Allied aircraft and two aircraft spotters.

29. Canadian infantry and armour street fighting in a village on the Falaise road.

30. ABOVE A Panzer IV, Ausführung H, knocked out during a rearguard action fought against 23rd Hussars of 11th Armoured Division, in Putanges on 18 August, 1944.

31. An assault gun (Sturmgeschütz) mounted on a Panzer III chassis and belonging to the 1st SS Panzer Division, pushed into the Orne after it ran out of petrol and had to be abandoned. (*Imperial War Museum*).

32. A Panther of 116th Panzer Division knocked out near St Germain Cathedral in Argentan.

33. A German soft-skinned vehicle column caught and set afire by aerial rocket and machine gun attack in a narrow lane.

34. ABOVE An aerial shot of the river Dives taken in 1975 and showing in the foreground the Moissy ford. Running from left to right across the picture is the St Lambert–Chambois road. Mount Ormel is just off the picture, top right. (*Courtesy of After the Battle*).

35. An aerial shot of the two bridges across the Dives at St Lambert taken during 1975. These are the two original bridges across which the German troops flooded past the Canadian group under Major Currie. (*Courtesy of After the Battle*).

battle line without officers, arms or equipment and it was only by such *ad hoc* measures that the line could be held at all. Army, aware of 84th Corps' weakness, authorized a further withdrawal to take place during the night of 14/15 August to a new line running from Mont Crespin to Larchamp. This was only an interim position anticipating a greater move back for which plans had already been formulated.

This step back during the night of the 16th was no less than 10 km deep and it was the most dramatic movement for its completion would bring Army east of the river Orne and would thus place a river defence line between the Germans and the pursuing Allies. There were, however, only a limited number of crossing points available. In 84th Corps sector there was only one bridge near Putanges and a shared bridge at St Croix across which the whole of Corps and 10th ss Panzer Division, which was placed under command for the withdrawal operation, would have to pass. To ease any possible congestion the whole movement was to be carried out during a period of three nights, beginning with that of 16/17 August. Every available officer, including the Corps Commander, was on the road controlling the convoys with such success that movement over the first bound was completed without congestion. In 84th Corps area, at least, the eastward flow had been smooth and regular.

For the infantry units of 3rd British Division fighting their way forward on the Vire-Flers road Wednesday 16 August was another day of bitter fighting and certainly the men on the ground were unaware that the pocket was deflating rapidly. Neither the men of British 8th Corps, around Flers, nor the Canadians fighting bitterly in the streets and houses of Falaise would have imagined that the Germans contesting every step of their advance were within a week of complete defeat. And yet, suddenly, on the morning of the 17th in front of 8th Corps resistance slackened as the German line thinned and moved back. Now the main resistance was in the cleverly placed mines, the blown bridges, the booby traps or the occasional sniper seizing a brief, unguarded moment to confuse and hinder the advance. Not until late in the afternoon were the leading elements of the British infantry to gain contact with the German rear-guards and from bushes and copses on the high ground, which sloped steeply down to the valley of the Orne, MG 42s and well-directed mortar fire brought to the pursuers the knowledge that the grenadiers of the German Army had reached another position which they were determined to hold.

On the American front forces from 1st Army had now reached the Army Group stop line and in obedience to orders halted and formed a strong front facing north. With the 1st Army halted the 3rd Army had, meanwhile, sent off armoured units in a relentless race to the Seine.

For the 17th the 84th Corps stood on the intermediate line, slowly detaching itself from the dogged grip of the pursuing British 2nd Army and filtering back across the Orne. Most of its units were posted to other Corps; 84th Division, excepting only a small battle group, went to the deep southern flank, 363rd Division had gone north to join II Para. Corps and only 353rd Division was still left under 84th Corps direct command.

The 7th Army ordered the evacuation across the Orne to be completed during the night of 17th/18th and Corps headquarters, now commanding only a single division, crossed the river and was placed at Army's disposal, awaiting its new and as yet unannounced role – the control of the final stages of the evacuation of the Falaise pocket.

The Southern Flank

'It is the Führer's Order.'
VON KLUGE TO HAUSSER, 9 August 1944

Even before the offensive to recapture Avranches had been launched it was becoming apparent that the southern flank was the one which would provoke the most serious situation. The delay in undertaking immediate measures to build the German southern wing can be attributed to many interrelated factors: the shortage of infantry and armour, the simultaneous attacks by the British and Canadians which tied down men and machines which might otherwise have been rushed to the threatened sector and the Allied command of the air which effectively halted all vehicular movement on the German side during the long hours of daylight and thus prevented a rapid switching of such forces which could be spared from the western salient.

Then, too, in view of Hitler's direct and rigid control of the Mortain offensive it would have shown lack of confidence, amounting to treason, on the part of von Kluge to have detached troops to deal with the southern threat. Hitler had, after all, forecast that the armoured spearheads of 3rd Army would wither and perish once they had been cut off from their supplies as a result of the closure of the gap at Avranches. It was a calculated risk which had to be taken that the Mortain offensive might very well bring this result about and if it did then its success would make the thrust to the south redundant.

The failure of the German counter-offensive to maintain its two-day time-table and reach the sea was obvious once the Typhoons, Spitfires and Thunderbolts had been let loose upon the columns and by their attacks had destroyed the German armoured spearheads. It was then that the thoughts of the senior commanders turned anxiously towards the open flank and one of the armoured units of the support wave, 10th ss Panzer Division 'Frundsberg', was detached and posted from the Mortain area for flank protection duties. This ss Division, raised only in December 1942, had garrisoned Marseilles and had then served on the Eastern Front in Tarnopol and in the northern Ukraine before returning with all despatch to the newly invaded Normandy. From late June and throughout July it had fought the British and now moved from the Odon front to bolster the under-manned southern sector.

The situation on that front was unclear. In the sector into which the Frundsberg Division moved it had not been established how far the American armoured units had driven, what villages and towns they had seized nor the strength, direction and intention of their assault. The battlefield conference

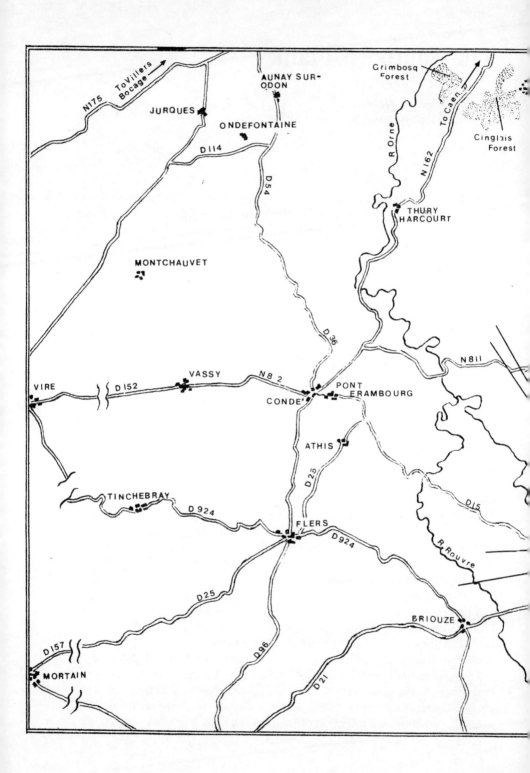

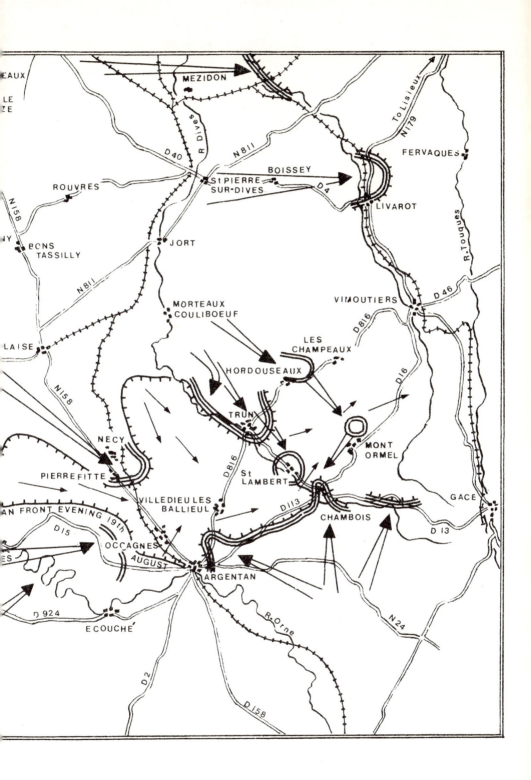

which sent the 10th ss Division's reconnaissance battalion out on a sweep along the Mortain–Domfront line could give little positive information. Somewhere to the south lay 275th Infantry Division, or so it was believed, and the reconnaissance battalion was ordered to gain touch with that unit. On the other hand the ss battalion might well find that the area had already been occupied by the American tank men. A second task as the ss battalion scouted the area which the division would occupy was to seize important road junctions and tactically important high ground which other divisional units would then occupy in strength.

It was in an atmosphere of uncertainty and doubt that the armoured car detachments swung southwards in the gathering dusk of 7 August and within kilometres had had their first brushes with onthrusting us tank forces. Barenton had already fallen and that strong American combat groups were heading towards the strategic road junction of Domfront was the alarming news which the results of their reconnaissances revealed. This meant that the us spearheads were located more than 20 km behind the German forces in Mortain and a change of direction northwards would inevitably cut off the German troops in that salient. At all costs the southern wing had to be secured. The 275th Infantry Division was no longer in a condition to establish and to maintain the strong defence which was needed and it was relieved from the line by 10th ss Panzer Division, which then went on to secure the heights north of Barenton and to block the roads and tracks leading to the north.

For the Allies 8 August had seen the development of a favourable situation. On 1st Army sector the Mortain offensive had been blocked, while to the south fast divisions of 3rd us Army were tearing their way round the German flank and advancing against only minimal resistance. This pleasing situation suggested to Bradley that changes might be made to the original Overlord concept and in the course of a telephone conversation with Montgomery he suggested that 15th us Corps, which had reached Laval and whose spearheads were nearly 100 km south east of Avranches, should change the direction of its advance from east to north. This 90° turn would menace the town of Alençon and threaten the entire German southern flank. Such an advance would fling a pincer arm around those German troops still concentrated in the Mortain salient and a simultaneous Canadian drive from the north and through Falaise to Argentan would form a second pincer. Within the steel grip of those two massive jaws the enemy forces would be completely destroyed. Montgomery approved Bradley's plan.

To Montgomery's logical mind the German Command in Normandy was faced with two bitter alternatives. Either it could reinforce defeat by building up its forces around Mortain or it could begin to move back towards the Seine and thus towards its fuel and ammunition supplies. Accepting that the latter course was the more likely one, Montgomery's appreciation of the situation was that 7th Army would concentrate its forces around Alençon so as to present a firm shoulder against the American northward drive. This advance they would further seek to delay by exploiting the natural advantages of ground found in the difficult bocage country in that sector. This build-up of the German southern wing must, he realized, weaken their hold on the northern flank and this would ease the Canadian advance. Thus it would be they and not the Americans who would first reach the town of Argentan where the British commander had planned that the Allied pincers would meet.

Although Montgomery realized the need to trap the German armies between the Loire and the Seine and had, indeed, planned for their destruction in that area, he appreciated that many might escape from the trap which he was casting for them. To catch these he planned a second and wider encirclement whose jaws would meet at the Seine and issued a directive setting out his intentions on 11 August. He was aware that the Allied air forces had destroyed many of the river bridges and that, therefore, the bulk of the two German armies would be unable to bring across the Seine the greatest part of their heavy equipment, guns and armour. Montgomery realized that he could move his armour faster than the Germans could withdraw and that his second pair of pincers would catch and crush against the Seine river barrier the great mass of the German armies in France.

*   *   *   *

While to the east of the rapidly forming pocket the 15th us Corps was driving towards Alençon the situation nearer to Mortain had become critical for the Germans. Preliminary moves had been made to detach the Panzer Group Eberbach and to set it against the threat coming up from the south. The 1st us Army was making a double-pronged push northwards towards the Army Group boundary and on the British and Canadian sectors heavy infantry fighting, prolonged artillery barrages and heavy air raids were sapping the strength of the German defenders. The 7th Army was almost isolated from the bulk of the German Army in the West and was also out of contact by telephone. There were shortages of everything; wirelesses, ammunition, spares for the armour, fuel for the vehicles and even of motor cycles for despatch riders. The Army had to undertake the dangerous task of using staff cars to carry messages between headquarters and those attracted the unwelcome attentions of Allied fighter bombers which ranged across the area.

Thus there could be no establishing of a firm front but rather the plugging of gaps through which American units filtered. One us unit suddenly appeared outside the town of Ger during 8 August and a hastily formed battle group had to be formed to drive it back. The 58th Panzer Corps ordered that the highway leading from Mortain to Domfront be cut to prevent the us forces from attaining the high ground between Barenton and St Georges. The 10th ss,

87

under Panzer Corps command, was to plan for the recapture of Barenton. The plans were laid and the 10th SS prepared itself for battle. Quickly and efficiently the SS units moved forward but they were not quick enough for even as the panzer and grenadier columns reached their forming up area they came under attack from US forces striking northwards to seize the hills upon which the SS had established their infantry outpost line. A three-pronged American assault came in under cover of an air umbrella, behind a heavy artillery barrage and led by an armoured wedge of sixty tanks. Against a detachment from the reconnaissance battalion one American unit assaulted and drove the SS from their positions on Point 266, a few kilometres north of Barenton. A second US battalion, attacking at the same time, drove up another hill and then the third American battalion struck Point 161 and took it. Behind the thin and loose line of strongpoints on the high ground the SS grenadiers and Engineers dug in around Rancoudray. The sudden and successful powerful US attack postponed the SS assault against Barenton and it did not go in until the morning of the 10th.

On that day it was the SS which struck the pre-emptive blow and caught the American armour before it had been able to deploy. Three columns of panzer-grenadiers from 22nd Regiment moved forward to storm the hills which had been lost on the previous day and to seize the divisional objective – Barenton. The battle which then followed was a completely new and shattering experience for the grenadiers. The fighting in which the division had been engaged, both in Russia and south of Caen, had been hard and had been made against armies whose units had a more lavish establishment than that which was available to the German armies at that stage of the war, but no experience had prepared the SS men for the prodigal expenditure of shells, tanks and aircraft which were put in to halt their attack.

Under the first German blow the US troops had withdrawn to regroup and, having reformed, contested every step of the SS advance. The grenadier columns raced to the base of Point 266 and began the ascent, breasting their way through machine gun and artillery fire, and bringing the advance slowly but steadily forward. Above the grenadiers labouring up the steep, grassy slopes there then emerged from cover squadrons of self-propelled guns which opened fire and brought the German infantry under direct fire at close range. The SS grenadiers went to ground and fired off the violet signal flares which indicated that they were under tank attack. Not far behind them, concealed in the bushes and trees of a small wood, were the panzers of the division's 2nd Battalion and in response to the infantry appeal the Panzer IVs and Vs rolled forward and engaged the US SP artillery. Column after column of smoke indicated where gun after gun had been caught, destroyed and was burning.

But the Americans had their own massive reserves of power upon which they called and brought forward the close-support fighter/bombers which flew low over the grenadier line, trying with high explosive and machine gun fire to stem the German assault. Box barrages were laid to contain and to destroy the grenadiers but these moved forward through the explosions, the bombardments and the machine gun fire to emerge at the top of Point 266, and in one last thrust to expel from its crest the American troops who had held it.

While the 22nd Regiment was making its final bid for the crest the divisional Engineer battalion poured down the slopes of Point 263, moved forward up the main road to Barenton and recaptured the village of Bousentier. But into the battle the Americans threw heavier air assaults and fiercer bombardments. Losses mounted and in the face of this overwhelming opposition the advance was finally brought to a halt less than 3 km from the objective. Between Barenton and Domfront lies the little village of St Georges and, during the time that 2nd Panzer Battalion and 22nd Grenadier Regiment had been attacking, the 21st Grenadier Regiment, on its sector around St Georges, had been under strong and constant pressure by a US armoured Combat Command striking northward from the village. The American thrust was covered by a mass of aircraft and large numbers of tanks which made a slow but sustained advance against the delaying tactics of the German outpost line.

After a forward movement of a little over 2 km the Americans came up against a firmer resistance and this was sufficient to hold back the advance. But the US pressure was maintained throughout 10 and 11 August, although on the German side the defence was now almost a totally infantry one. The divisional armour had been reduced to only ten vehicles and the artillery had fired off most of its ammunition. The defence of the southern wing then depended upon the courage and skill of the grenadiers who with panzerfaust were ordered to hold the furious armoured assaults which would be certain to be launched upon them.

The exhausted grenadiers were soon put to the test when following a long barrage of terrible dimensions a sudden, furious assault was flung in against them during the morning of the 12th. American artillery shells tore apart platoons of men, strong points were smashed and the whole front line of the Frundsberg grenadiers obliterated under a storm of shellfire. Behind the barrage came the armour, machine gunning and 'flaming' any resistance and behind the armour followed the waves of infantry to mop up and to consolidate the gains.

All day long the desperate resistance was maintained. The order from 58th Panzer Corps had been crystal clear; the southern flank had to be held at all costs. Small groups of grenadiers, survivors from the shelling, the 'flamings', the aerial assault and the machine guns of the US infantry assembled, rearmed, regrouped and stormed forward into hopeless counter-attacks. Their losses were high. By the end of 12 August the 21st Grenadier Regiment had been reduced to only 500 men, while the sister regiment could muster only 250.

Eight tanks were still fit for action, the artillery regiment had been reduced to only twenty-five pieces, including eight self-propelled guns. The division had shrunk to less than the strength of a single regiment. It was clear that under such losses the Division could no longer maintain its positions and a withdrawal northwards brought its units to an interim line running from Placite to Lonlay, where the Division rested, generally undisturbed, for the whole of 13 August, before continuing the rearward movement, during the night of the 14th, to a new line behind the Egrenne river.

To von Kluge the thrust which the Americans were making in their drive via Alençon towards Argentan, had struck 7th Army in the flank and, taken in conjunction with Canadian pressure on the Laison river, showed how the pocket had developed in which his forces were held. As early as 10 August von Kluge had proposed that the forces concentrated to renew the attack upon Avranches should strike southwards at 15th US Corps. This matter had become one of the gravest importance for German 81st Corps had been shattered by the advance of 15th US Corps. The Americans had struck forward between Alençon and Argentan and by threatening the vast petrol and supply dumps in that sector had precipitated a crisis within the salient extending back to Mortain. The American Corps commander, Haislip, appreciating that the vast Forêt d'Ecouves might well conceal German reserves ordered that his two armoured divisions, 2nd French and 5th US, were to bypass the forest to the west and east respectively. The French commander then was guilty of an astonishing piece of military bad manners. In order to bring his units that much more quickly into position he trespassed upon one of the roads reserved for the 5th US Armoured Division and blocked the highway to such effect that the advance of 5th Armoured was delayed for nearly half a day. It had been the task of the Americans to bring the advance towards Argentan along with maximum speed but the French obstruction allowed Eberbach to bring forward elements of 116th Panzer Division to take up strong defensive positions from which it was able to delay and finally to halt the US drive.

Until that time the American attack had flown smoothly forward and Haislip, 15th Corps Commander, made a proposal to Patton. His orders from 3rd Army Commander had been that he was to advance his Corps towards the Army Group boundary but Patton's conversation then went on to mention a 'further advance' beyond that point. Haislip was convinced that the objective of Argentan lay within his grasp – that he had a force strong enough to hold any ground that he could capture but suggested that more troops placed under his command could be used to cut the east/west German escape routes. He proposed and Patton authorized a slow advance towards Falaise; the junior commander suggesting and his superior assenting to an American incursion into the British/Canadian sector and aimed at the capture of the town of Argentan.

This was a new example of military bad manners which could have had more serious implications than the French trespass. It will be appreciated that in the course of military operations boundaries are allotted to formations and that these divide the ground that roads of advance and withdrawal are apportioned. It also follows that the larger the formation then the more firmly fixed must be its boundaries. In the interests of efficiency it is vital that boundaries once fixed are adhered to and designated roads left to that unit through whose territory they run.

The boundary line between the 12th US Army Group and 21st British Army Group ran south of Argentan and thus placed that town within the British/Canadian sector. In his appreciation of the situation Montgomery had anticipated that the Canadians would reach the town before 15th US Corps but the defence by the SS on the northern sector had slowed the Canadian advance to such a degree that it was the Americans who were now nearing the town. Nevertheless, Montgomery did not move the Army Group boundary – a decision which was to be widely criticised – and Patton had allowed Haislip to cross it. French patrols had entered the town during the 13th but had then moved back to allow the 5th US Armoured Division to take the town completely. But before the first units of that division could move forward Eberbach had established his strong defence line south of the town and had halted the American advance.

*   *   *

This chapter has already shown several instances of a lack of military judgment connected with the Falaise battle. There was the false appreciation by Montgomery of the Canadian drive towards Argentan, the French *fait accompli* on the roads up to the Forêt d'Ecouves and the American encroachment into the British/Canadian area. Now there was to be a new move and one which has subsequently caused more recrimination among the Allied military than almost any other comparable decision; Bradley halted the advance across the Army Group boundary.

When he became aware that Haislip's Corps had made its trespass he immediately ordered Patton to stop all northward movement and, during the afternoon of 13 August, 3rd Army commander transmitted that order to his Corps commander. The American force was halted south of Argentan.

The reasons for Bradley's actions were sound military ones and although others were added in later years, to justify his decision, there is little doubt that his action, with the information he had, was the right one.

It will be remembered that Bradley, although now equal in status to Montgomery as an Army Group commander, was still subordinate to the British commander who was in charge of the tactical situation. In Bradley's estimation it was not for him to suggest that the Army Group boundary be moved and then there was the second point that south of the town of Argentan

Haislip's 15th Corps had begun to meet increasing and stronger resistance. Then, too, there was a wide gap on the left flank of 15th Corps and it would have been militarily unsound to allow a unit to advance against a strong enemy with one of its flanks uncovered.

Into the gap on the left flank of 15th Corps there slowly filtered the leading elements of 7th Corps but then came confusion as more and more American units crowded into the confined space on the southern flank. The 20th US Corps also began to move up on Haislip's left and two of its units collided in their advance with two of his divisions, the 90th Infantry and 2nd French Armoured. As more and more 7th Corps troops came into the line so the 20th was pinched out and was available for redeployment on another sector.

Feeling that the southern flank was now secure Bradley detached part of 15th Corps and sent it eastwards toward Dreux and the Seine. The reasons which influenced his decision included the fact that the German 81st Corps had been badly hit, that there seemed to be few German troops between Argentan and the Seine and the faulty American intelligence which had estimated that the bulk of 7th Army and 5th Panzer Army had already escaped from the pocket. In his assumption that the Canadian offensive was moving too slowly to catch the remaining German forces and conscious of the option expressed in Montgomery's directive of 11 August to provide for a larger encirclement along the river Seine, he forgot, however, to inform Montgomery of his action.

With Haislip's 5th Armoured Division and 79th Infantry Division detached and heading for Dreux there was now only a skeleton and provisional Corps in the Alençon area to control 2nd French Armoured Division, the 90th and 80th US Infantry Divisions. Then on 15 August Patton detached part of 90th Division from its area at Le Bourg St Léonard, east of Argentan, and sent it flying off to seize Gacé and to cut the escape routes to Lisieux, Bernay and Rouen.

* * *

To von Kluge the threat on the southern flank was rapidly approaching a crisis situation and he considered that the time was ripe for a drive against the open flank of 15th US Corps. In his favour were the facts that the Canadian offensive on the northern side of the pocket had been slowed and held by the almost fanatical resistance offered by 12th SS Panzer Division and while his northern flank held and the western one was still able to resist the Allied pressure then he was free to deal with the situation in the south. Discreetly he began to assemble and to regroup his armoured forces waiting for the authority to begin his counter-offensive which could only come from Adolf Hitler.

The search for units available for the offensive was a difficult one. The Panzer Group Eberbach was in no position to undertake an offensive, even though it had recently taken on strength the 9th Panzer Division from southern France. In any case his force had been ordered to take up positions south of Argentan and his 116th Panzer Division had already moved to hold back the slowly advancing troops of 15th US Corps.

Von Kluge finished the reshuffle of his panzer forces and ordered an attack against the Americans to go in on 14 August. The forces were to include 1st SS Panzer Division, the 2nd Panzer, 116th Panzer, the 10th SS Panzer and were to be supported by two brigades of heavy and super-heavy mortars as well as a heavy artillery battalion. The 116th Panzer Division was in Argentan, 2nd Panzer in the Ecouche area, the 1st SS 'Leibstandarte' between Carrouges and La Ferté-Macé and the whole Panzer Group now controlled a force of only seventy armoured fighting vehicles. Despite the few vehicles available the determined actions of the Panzer Group formations held the southern front intact, in their own area. Along other sectors of that flank the armour which Hitler had ordered to join Eberbach had been siphoned off by 7th Army to plug the gaps in the line which were appearing as a result of the growing Allied pressure.

The first indications of this on the southern front came in a general and concerted attack on 14 August against the 10th SS Panzer Division. During the late morning a combined US armoured and infantry attack was made towards the hills to the north and to the north west of Domfront. Against the squadrons of tanks which the Americans put into the battle the Frundsberg panzer regiment could commit only eight machines, the last remnants of its two panzer battalions.

An SS principle had always been that boldness and attack would defeat a hesitant and defensively minded foe. It was in the spirit of that belief that Harmel, GOC of 10th SS Panzer Division, brought together a handful of grenadier platoons, borrowed artillery ammunition from other SS divisions and decided upon a limited attack which would thrust into the American flank and fling back from the valley of the Egrenne river those armoured spearheads of the US forces which had entered it. Shortly after noon the final preparations had been completed and the artillery tasks allotted. The guns had not only to support the grenadier assault, but also to drive back any counter-attack, protect the flanks of the attack and cut off from relief the Americans against whom the Frundsbergs were to make their pre-emptive blow.

At 14.00 hrs a bombardment began. By the standards of American gun-fire this was no heavy barrage but it was stronger than any which the Germans had been able to fire throughout the past weeks. Small and of short duration though it was, it was still powerful enough to surprise and drive to ground the US troops who had been advancing into the hilly country north of Domfront.

Behind the barrage the last eight panzers rolled forward bearing, clustered around their turrets, platoons of grenadiers. On through the counter-barrage, across the rolling ground they rumbled, firing to such effect that the stronger American force shrank back and withdrew.

For the time being the bold ss stroke had halted the Allied drive and had dominated the situation. Not for long, however, for pressure built up again during 15 August, forcing a further withdrawal, covered by an aggressive rearguard, back to St Bomer-les-Forges, on either side of which the divisional fragments dug in to defend themselves once again. This rearward movement was not to be completed without incident, for during the fore-noon of 15 August, an armoured group stormed out Domfront and attacked the withdrawing German units. The whole area was covered with high bushes and trees within the cover of which the us vehicles and men of the advanced guard detachments were able to hide and to pour fire upon the groups of grenadiers heading for their new positions. Short battles brewed up as the ss men turned at bay, fighting the Shermans and the armoured personnel carriers with rocket launchers and with hollow-charge grenades. The ss anti-tank battalion rushed forward the last remaining, undamaged guns and camouflaged them in the bushes and hedgerows, covering every approach across the area through which the American task force would have to pass.

Then, all of a sudden, the main body of the American force struck across the close country and into point blank range. The ss anti-tank guns, supported by the few remaining panzers, opened up. American tanks began to burn, others halted with their tracks shattered and in the confusion the us artillery observers, unable through the thick undergrowth to distinguish friend from foe, covered their own halted advance with a crashing artillery bombardment. The mistake was soon righted but barely had the barrage lifted than the ss grenadiers stormed forward with machine pistols and grenades driving back the dismounted American infantry. Where resistance was met a shower of rifle grenades or a barrage of mortar bombs helped to break it. Immobile American tanks were searched for usable equipment before being blown up. Soon it was all over and the withdrawal was completed without further interruption.

During the course of the day orders were received from Corps removing 10th ss Division from the line. Army Group 'B' had planned that a mobile panzer strike force was to be assembled and placed under command of 5th Panzer Army. Panzer Group Eberbach was thereupon struck off 7th Army strength and placed on that of 5th Panzer Army. It was to be the role of this counter-attack group to meet and to destroy those American tank thrusts which, by striking northwards in the Putanges area, were drawing a noose tight around the German armies. The panzer force's main task would be to hold back the us armour until the planned withdrawal of the main strength of 7th Army across the Dives river had been accomplished and the Army had been brought out of the pocket.

The relief of any unit from the line is never easy but the relief of a unit locked in battle is one which consumes time, energy and patience. The difficulties which were connected with the withdrawal of 10th ss from its positions were such that it was not until shortly before first light on the 16th that the last detachments of grenadiers moved back into the rear areas. By late in the morning the marching columns had reached the new forming up location around Saires-le-Verrière.

The tribulations of 10th ss did not end with its concentration in the forming up ground for orders then came that it was to move again, to a point north of the threatened town of Argentan where the counter-attack force was being gathered. For the new move the ss Division came, temporarily, under command of 84th Corps which, it will be remembered, had been given control of movements across the Orne, and was ordered to make for the bridge at Putanges. Pressure against Corps' left wing during the day forced the withdrawal of the threatened flank and both Briouze, on the Flers–Argentan road, and the little village of Bellau-en-Houlme fell to the Americans. The fall of those two places thus placed American armoured units athwart the roads along which the ss had been ordered to march to the new area and the Frundsberg Division, which had believed itself to have been relieved from the line, would have to fight its way through at least two American armoured groups in order to reach and hold the Orne bridge before the us troops could cut it off.

The Division was deployed for battle and swung out a pincer arm made up of the Engineer battalion, now only 300 men strong, to take Bellau-en-Houlme from the north while the grenadier regiments moved frontally against the place. Across the countryside thickly set with bushes of gorse and other weeds the depleted companies moved forward. They were few in number now and almost unsupported by the artillery, for the guns had lost so many men and prime movers that they could not bring the pieces forward. As the grenadiers covered the ground using the tactics of fire and movement to open the attack, the few self-propelled guns still with the artillery regiment were switched from sector to sector to beat down the American opposition and to support the forward movement of their own infantry companies.

American opposition was strong and the us soldiers determined but the Frundsberg grenadiers knew that they had to win this attack if they were to survive and flung themselves forward through artillery barrages, up to and across and then through the American infantry positions, bombing their way forward and by the spirit of their charge driving the us soldiers back, recapturing Bellau and La Ferminiere, a small hamlet to the south of the village. Once through the American blocks the grenadiers did not continue with their advance but were swung in a right wheel and dug in forming a chain of defensive positions facing southwards. For the time being their action had halted the American northward drive and was holding 15th us Corps at bay. Forming 10th Division's left flank was the reconnaissance battalion, of 9th ss

Panzer Division, whose front covered the area from Putanges via Ecouche to Argentan. The 9th ss had also been ordered to concentrate north of Argentan but during the day a wireless message was received cancelling the orders for the grouping of a counter-attack force. The strength of the units which would have made up the group had been continually reduced by losses and Panzer Group Eberbach, posted from 7th Army and placed directly under control of Army Group 'B', no longer had the strength to carry out the tasks which would face it. As an example of the weakness of its units the 9th Panzer Division had been reduced to the strength of a single panzer company and the other formations were in no better shape.

Shortages of petrol, lack of spares, vehicle and crew losses had all combined to weaken the proposed force and only a powerful grouping used en masse would have had the power to halt the us thrusts. So strong had these become and so weak the Panzer Group that the High Command War Diary recorded that in its first engagement the Eberbach formation had been forced to take up a defensive posture. In view of this it was generally accepted that only an immediate withdrawal out of the encirclement by a thrust in a north-westerly direction could save the trapped armies.

Faulty Allied Intelligence had stated that the bulk of the German forces in the pocket had made their way eastwards and had thus escaped encirclement along the line of the Orne. During 16 August Montgomery proposed to Bradley that the Canadian and the American forces meet, not at Argentan but in the area between Trun and Chambois, that is along the line of the river Dives. It was hoped that there the fleeing 7th Army, or so everybody believed it to be, could be caught before it escaped in the high country at Vimoutiers.

A factor which influenced Montgomery was that the divisions which Haislip had left behind to close the gap by linking with the Canadians pushing down from Falaise did not have the strength to move against the German forces still holding the jaws of the Allied pincers apart. The 90th us Infantry Division had, in fact, been rather badly mauled at St Léonard when elements of 2nd ss Panzer and 116th Panzer Divisions had mounted a local attack and had, temporarily, driven the Americans out of the place.

Acting upon Montgomery's proposal Bradley gave orders to Patton, whose attention was now fixed upon reaching the Seine, to send divisions to seize both Chambois and Trun and, thereby, to link up with the Canadians. It will be remembered that in the Alençon area there was only a provisional Corps. To control operations in the Alençon sector Patton sent his Chief of Staff, Gaffey, to supervise the development of operations around Argentan. The 2nd French Armoured Division was ordered to send a Combat Command forward west of Argentan to cut the Argentan–Falaise road, the 90th Division was given the task of capturing Chambois, a second French Combat Command was to take Trun and in this operation was to be supported by the 80th us Division. The operations were timed to begin on 17 August.

Then into the arena came a new figure. General Gerow, whose 5th US Corps had been pinched out near Tinchebrai on 15 August, was sent two days later to Alençon to take command of the provisional Corps there. Bradley had altered the boundary between 1st and 3rd US Armies without informing Patton and had placed the Argentan sector within the area of 1st Army. This would, as he saw it, leave 3rd Army free to head in strength to the Seine.

The new Corps Commander, Gerow, postponed the attack which his predecessor Gaffey had intended to open on the 17th and until the arrival of 5th Corps artillery en route from Tinchebrai. As a pre-requisite for the success of the attack Gerow insisted upon the recapture of St Léonard, so as to secure jump-off positions. During the night of 17/18 August the 90th US Division went in and against only light opposition seized the town from 2nd SS Panzer Division which was withdrawing to join the SS Panzer Corps at Vimoutiers.

Along other sectors of the pocket Allied pressure against the Germans grew. The British 12th Corps had reached a point halfway along the Falaise–Argentan road, 90th Division was nearing Chambois, the 4th Canadian Armoured Division was nearing St Lambert, the Poles had captured certain strategically important hills near Hordouseaux and had sent reconnaissance troops towards Trun. The 2nd French Armoured Division was holding the Ecouché–Argentan road and 80th Division had cut the Argentan–Trun road.

As the Allies pressed in upon the hard-fighting German divisions there was a slow but maintained reduction in the size of the pocket. Lack of signals equipment to pass wireless messages, lack of physical contact with neighbouring units and the unnecessary calls to action prevented news of the grave situation in which the armies were placed being generally known. The battalions locked in battle on the Falaise sector knew as little of the overall picture or of the fighting which was being carried out from Domfront to Argentan, as did those defenders of the eastward thrusts of the Canadian Corps across the Dives river. None of the grenadier and panzer units fighting their desperate, rearguard battles, mounting their small counter-attacks or cowering in their slit trenches as artillery bombardments shook the ground and destroyed every standing thing, was aware that behind the wall which their bravery was maintaining had begun and was continuing an evacuation of their armies.

From the high ground we could sometimes see Allied Jabos [fighter/bombers] roaring low firing rockets and machine gunning away behind us. We did not know what were their targets but we thought that they were probably transport columns. I suppose that in some malicious way we were pleased that the rear area troops were getting a taste of real war, the sort we had been fighting and, anyway, if the Jabos were attacking them, they were leaving us alone.

During the night of 16/17 August, 10th ss came, once again, under pressure as it moved towards the Orne bridge at Putanges taking with it, in its rearward movement, the reconnaissance battalion of 9th ss Panzer Division. The American advance guards, keen to strike more quickly into the pocket, pressed forward and threatened to overrun in their advance the Frundsberg rearguard, made up of the last companies of the divisional Engineer battalion. At Fromentel part of the us point unit struck forward too boldly and without its back-up units. Always watching to seize the tactical chances which such mistakes offered the Engineer battalion halted, formed a front and with the support of the last armoured fighting vehicles, eight machines all told, waited for the Shermans to charge.

The us armour breasted the rise to face, waiting on the reverse slope, the small German detachment. The first shots brought the leading troops to a halt and as the supporting infantry went to ground, the grenadier mortar teams fired a short but intense and accurate barrage. The us armour and infantry streamed back over the hill leaving burning vehicles to mark the small success which the ss Engineers had won. The American enthusiasm to destroy the weakening Germans on that sector was, temporarily, dampened.

Orders from 84th Corps came in during the late afternoon of the 17th specifying Division's boundaries during the coming night and giving details for the crossing of the Orne by the Menil bridge. Behind a rear-guard mounted by the reconnaissance battalion Frundsberg crossed the river, reporting only slight interference from American artillery fire and a minimum of obstruction from other units using the bridge in their eastward movement. The withdrawal was still proceeding in a reasonably smooth and orderly fashion and although taking place at night showed no signs of the confusion into which it later was to degenerate.

By dawn on 18 August the 10th ss had crossed the Orne, the rear-guard had been brought back and had been allotted new duties to protect the back of the main body as the divisional units moved towards the new form-up area at Habloville.

Only the marching columns and the remaining artillery pieces reached the new area; the last tanks were sent to Nécy on the northern flank and the divisional train was taken entirely out of the pocket. As they marched the grenadiers could see the destruction which the Allied aircraft and artillery fire had caused.

There were vehicles burning at intervals along the road and from every narrow country road lorries, sometimes just one machine, sometimes a whole convoy of lorries would try to edge their way into the main columns. After a number of miles the whole width of the road was completely filled.

Until then part of the road had been kept clear for vehicles with special duties, ambulances, despatch riders and the like. But during the climb up from the Orne valley faster moving lorries had tried to overtake the slower vehicles and had then formed two, and then three columns of traffic.

To add to the confusion Allied fighter/bombers swooped down in destructive assaults for as long as there was light enough to see the slow-moving traffic and each fresh attack brought with it new destruction and greater congestion which slowed the pace of the retreat. The infantry and those vehicles which were not tied to roads and tracks made their way across country where this was possible but were often caught on the open ground and either destroyed outright or shepherded back to the cover of the trees on the main road and attacked there. The columns were subject not only to repeated, almost continuous, aerial assault. Far away to the south American heavy guns had been brought up into position and from points miles removed from the pocket had opened up intermittent long-range bombardments upon every road and track.

> We cursed the little dark-green, high-wing aeroplanes. We knew that one of them in the area would precede a barrage and we tried our hardest to shoot them down. If we gave them too hard a time they were impudent enough to fire off a few flares and call up the Typhoons to 'rocket' us. We dreaded those little observation aeroplanes – they were the angels of death to us.

Under such difficult conditions it was hardly surprising that it was not until midday on 19 August that the widely separated and shattered columns of 10th ss Panzer Division, having crossed the Falaise–Argentan highway, ascended the steep hills and passed into the protection of the great woods of Gouffern, began the descent towards the valley of the river Dives and the concentration area of Villedieu-les-Ballieul, before making the last bound that would have taken them outside the pocket.

It is here that we leave the 10th ss Panzer Division and its defence of the southern flank. Before we cross the whole width of the pocket to describe the fighting which had taken place on the northern flank let us see how the situation had developed on other sectors of the front.

The 80th us Division, fighting its way forward to cut the Argentan–Trun road, was meeting fierce resistance, the 90th, to which had been given the task of cutting the St Léonard–Chambois road, was held in the Forêt de Gouffen by 116th Panzer Division and the 8th Heavy Mortar Brigade. The 58th Panzer Corps and elements of the 116th were escaping eastwards and were having to run the gauntlet of Allied artillery fire.

On the British sector 30th Corps had crossed the Orne and was nearing the Falaise–Argentan road. A small Canadian force was in St Lambert – like a rock in a sea of German units which swept past on either side of it. Other Canadians were in Moissy and there was an armoured brigade in the Hordouseaux–Ecorches area. The 3rd Canadian Division was blocking the escape routes between Beauvais and Trun and the 4th Canadian Division was blocking the Trun–Vimoutiers road between Trun and Hordouseaux. With the Poles dominating the high ground in the Chambois–Vimoutiers road area the net was completely cast and there remained only the physical link-up which would cut off from all hope of escape those German troops still held within it.

The Northern Flank

'During the night of 18/19 August, the enemy found a gap which he exploited and rolled over divisional headquarters.'
H. MEYER, GS01, 12th SS Panzer Division

Into the area to the north of Falaise during the first week of August were concentrated the remnants of 12th SS Panzer Division 'Hitler Youth'. This newly raised formation had undergone its baptism of fire west of Caen and over a period of time which extended from D-Day until the beginning of July. Within those few short weeks this élite, first class, armoured division had been all but destroyed. Now the panzer regiment's two tank battalions were both under strength. From the amalgamation of three battalions of 25th Panzer Grenadier Regiment had been created the 'Waldmuller' battle group and a battle group 'Krause' had been formed from the amalgamation of the battalions of 26th Panzer Grenadier Regiment. The artillery component was two weak gun and one rocket battalion. In addition to the standard reconnaissance troops, Engineers, anti-tank, flak groups and two platoons of grenadiers forming the divisional headquarters company, there had come on to strength a company of self-propelled 3.7 cm anti-tank guns. But not a single grenadier had been received to replace the infantry which had been lost during the past weeks of battle.

The bloody sacrifice of 'Hitler Youth' Division had helped to hold the Canadians and the British and had stopped them from achieving one of the principal objectives of D-Day, the capture of Caen. When on 9 July that city passed into British hands the shattered 'Hitler Youth' Division had been at last withdrawn from the line but was then sent back in again and fought until it was relieved by 272nd Division. The 12th SS then moved to an area north of Falaise on ground which was to be directly in the path of the Canadians thrusting southwards in two operations codenamed 'Totalize' and 'Tractable' aimed at the capture of the nodal point of the town of Falaise, south east of Caen, for the capture of that place was a pre-requisite to the great drive to the Seine.

It had been planned that 12th SS in the forthcoming battle would be a counter-attack force for, although weak, the 'Hitler Youth' was by no means powerless and its grenadiers although tired had lost little of their fighting spirit and had gained a wealth of combat experience.

Against the thin line, held on that Falaise road sector by 89th and 271st Infantry Divisions, and which had the 12th SS in support, were to be flung during the impending battles the full force of the 1st Canadian Army, which

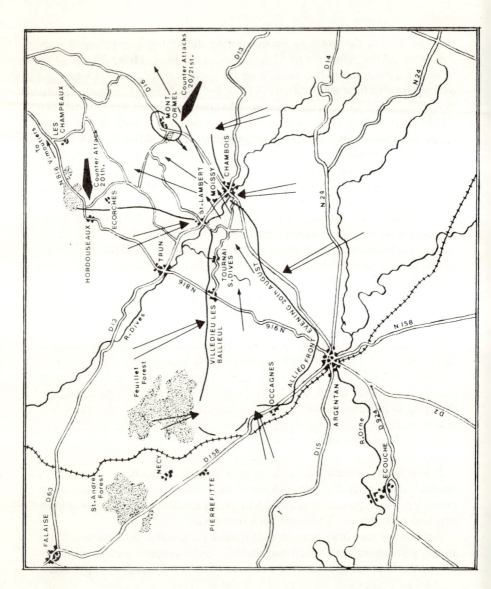

included 51st Highland Division, 4th Canadian Armoured Division, two Canadian armoured brigades and 2nd Canadian Infantry Division. At a later stage 1st Polish Armoured Division would also take part in the battles. General Simonds, 2nd Canadian Corps commander, planned for armoured phalanxes in line abreast to sweep southwards in a night attack across country and over an enemy which would have been crushed under massive aerial bombardments. Falaise would fall during the late afternoon of the first day of the offensive.

So far as the ss was concerned the battle opened to the west of the Falaise road during the evening of 6 August when British 59th Division and 34th Tank Brigade established a bridgehead across the Orne river above Thury-Harcourt. This bridgehead meant that the flank of the German troops in the Falaise sector might be turned. The Krause battle group of 12th ss Division was detached and ordered to collaborate with 89th Division in an attack to destroy the British lodgement. The 89th Division was in a poor state. It lacked armoured support and was without heavy anti-tank guns; its artillery was entirely horse-drawn and it had no mobile reserve. It was typical of the divisions which were being committed to the defence of Normandy during the early autumn of 1944.

Made wise by the frequent and destructive air attacks by Spitfires and Typhoons upon their vehicles the ss grenadiers spaced out their motorized convoys and, for greater concealment, drove through the Cinglais woods via St Laurent and then into the Grimbosq woods heading for the bridgehead sector. Deep within this forest their advance was contested and they dismounted from the carriers and tanks, shook out into battle formation and made their way between the trees beating back the British outposts which had already penetrated into the forest area. Along the rides and in the copses fire broke out but the hard-won battle skills of the ss grenadiers coupled with their indoctrinated ruthlessness forced back the British infantry and expelled them from the woods. Then, as the ss troopers emerged from under the trees their thin fighting line was hidden in a hurricane of explosions, smoke and flame from a barrage which fell upon it with deadly accuracy. No soldiers could advance through such a bombardment. The ss retired into the woods, reformed, and then struck forward again, moving this time in artillery formation through the British barrage and up the slope towards the village of Grimbosq before going on to strike at the bridgehead. But for all their *élan* they were too few in number to destroy it; they could only reduce its extent. The battle group then positioned itself around the north-eastern flank of the British incursion. A roll call showed how heavy had been the fighting for the ss losses in dead had been enormous and there was scarcely a man who did not have some wound.

The Waldmuller battle group still held the divisional line behind and to the east of the 89th Division but the projected divisional task of forming a counter-attack group was now no longer feasible for half the strength of the Division was now miles away and deeply committed in the fighting at Thury-Harcourt.

The ground operation of Totalize began at 21.30 hrs on Tuesday 8 August when the massed Canadian armour attacked on a narrow front on either side of the Caen–Falaise road. Together with the barrage that the Royal Artillery was firing the gunners of the light anti-aircraft batteries fired tracer shells from their Bofors guns to indicate direction to the attacking forces. To lighten the darkness searchlights were shone on to the clouds and the reflected rays created a sort of artificial moonlight.

Smoke shells fired upon the German positions hid from the eyes of the 89th Division's observers the great columns of armour roaring four abreast towards them. The armour struck at and then through the battle line of that unfortunate German formation. With little pause the Shermans rolled over the field defences but this is not to say that the whole Division was destroyed in a single blow. Here and there small pockets of infantry held out and delayed the Allied advance while a sketchy defence line was formed behind them. The ss grenadiers were brought to instant readiness. Their commander, Panzermeyer, had had orders to block the Canadian advance down the Falaise road and he could see that the lie of the land favoured the defence. To the north of Falaise and starting from the left of the Caen road the ground began slowly to flatten and to open into a type of heathland which extended eastwards to St Pierre-sur-Dives. The valley of the river Dives formed a natural tank barrier and the heights at Potigny were another bastion. Through Potigny village ran east–west and north–south roads and thus whoever held the place controlled the advance. Farther north there was another natural barrier, the small village of Cintheaux standing on the 127 m contour line and dominating the road from Bourguebus. Cintheaux was the forward defence sector of Potigny just as that place was the forward defence of Falaise. These localities would, therefore, form the blocks to obstruct the Allied thrust but the ss must advance and seize those places before the Canadian and Polish armour, supporting the 2nd Division on the western side of the road and 51st Highland Division on the eastern side of the road, could reach them.

Every man must be collected to hold the line and the vital area was now the Falaise road and not the bridgehead at Thury-Harcourt. Orders went out to the Krause battle group to return with best possible speed to the divisional sector. There they were to attain the heights at Potigny and were to defend the area between the Laison and the Laize rivers. To the Waldmuller group was given the task of knocking the Canadian attack off balance. It was to go in with a divisional panzer battalion and the remnants of 501 Tiger Tank Battalion, a Corps troops formation, to seize Cintheaux and then to go on to attack and capture the Garcelles woods. Then it was to reach the heights south of St

Aignan de Cramesnil. To the divisional headquarters defence company and
the self-propelled anti-tank guns was given the task of driving forward to
capture the uplands west of St Sylvain. If all these objectives were attained
then the 12th ss would be lying along a line roughly south west to north east
and covering not only the vital road but also the open heath country which led
to the Vie river. With the high ground north of Falaise firmly in their
possession they would gain time for a strong battle line to be manned behind
them. The Grenadiers were not yet aware that upon their fighting ability
would depend, within a few weeks, the fate of a greater part of the German
Army in the West although they thought that the situation was grave.

It was made known to us that we would have to fight as we had not fought
before because this new Canadian offensive would be a major operation.
We were, of course, tired from weeks of hard campaigning but we felt that
we had the measure of the Canadians and that their armoured effort would
be as slow and ponderous as usual. This we could deal with for the terrain
with its many bushes, cultivated ground and hedges favoured the defence
and particularly the two-man tank busting teams which we had formed. We
knew that we could hold.

Cintheaux was dominated by a large farm and into the area east of that
complex of buildings moved Wittmann's 501st Tiger Tank Battalion, a force
now shrunken to only fifty vehicles. Michael Wittmann was a tank fighter
whose single-handed exploit against 22nd British Armoured Brigade at
Villers-Bocage on 13 June had made him a legend among the soldiers of
Army Group 'B'. With Wittmann and his Tigers close at hand the grenadiers
could feel confident that in the coming battle they would be well supported.
En route to his forming up place he had already engaged and destroyed a
vedette of Canadian tanks and now, hidden in copses and buildings in and
around the farm, his tanks waited for orders to move.

The divisional commander watching the Canadian advance saw how the
hundreds of vehicles had been formed into massive and undeployable blocks
of armour. One square was approaching up the road to Bretteville-sur-Laize,
others were moving below Garcelles and out of the great woods to the south of
that place more columns were emerging and rolling forward. The Waldmuller
group and the Wittmann panzer group would have to beat back the Canadians
through the Garcelles woods if they were to carry out Panzermeyer's orders.
But then as the commander looked the pace of the Canadian advance slowed
and then halted as if the columns were uncertain of what they were to do next.
The ss leader did not know that the Allied bomber formations were on their
way to 'soften up' the enemy in front of the Canadian armour; he took the
tank delay for caution and decided to launch a pre-emptive attack which
would counter the advance.

His plan was simple. Cintheaux farm would be held by the minimum number of grenadiers – every soldier who could be spared would be put into the attack to the far east of the road. Quickly the orders were given, tasks allotted and boundaries defined. The attack would roll at 12.30 hrs.

Wittmann was a silent and introspective man and his battle orders were, as usual, brief and to the point. The attack would advance from the reverse slope behind which his machines were hidden and would drive with all speed so as to be in among the enemy and confuse him. Through earphones he heard the reports of his forward observation group. Suddenly he waved his arm and above the rumbling of the Allied bombardment there rose the harsh and strident roar of tank machines. Wittmann spoke into the intercom mouth-piece 'Panzer – marsch' and from out of their concealment the 56 one-ton Tigers rolled forward, moved up the slight slope, over the crest and down the incline on the enemy side of the hill, driving fast and in shallow wedge formation, using every fold in the ground which afforded protection and by a combination of fire and movement bringing the advance forward. At 1800 m the long-barrelled 8.8 cm guns fired. With a muzzle velocity of 810 m/sec. the shells could penetrate 10.8 cm of steel at that range and the Allied tanks were being destroyed at distances beyond those of their own main armament. Clinging to the outsides of tanks or mounted in armoured personnel carriers were the grenadiers accompanying the panzer thrust, holding on to stanchions as the vehicles plunged and bucketed their way across the open ground. The pace of the advance accelerated to maximum speed, 38 kmh; the panzers fanned out into attack formation and the ss infantry stood ready to leap from their vehicles and crush the Canadians by conventional ground assault. The armoured carriers passed through the thundering, crushing barrage but were then forced to halt in the shelter of the trees. The young men leapt from the machines, forming up under fire and following their officers who, pistol in hand, led the advance of the thin grey grenadier line steadily forward through the confusion of the Allied artillery fire.

Flying high above the battlefield came Allied bombers, for whose arrival the Canadian armoured phalanxes had waited, making for their principal target, the Cintheaux farm. An immediate evacuation of that place and of the target area was ordered by the ss commander. It would have been madness to stay and risk unnecessary casualties. Once the bombers had dropped their loads and if the Canadians were as hesitant in following behind this bombing raid as they had shown themselves usually to be, then the grenadiers could race forward and occupy the farm complex and take it firmly into German hands again. 'The Americans were not selective and they bombed the whole area around the farm. Villages and single houses were smashed. The air was filled with a fine white dust from the destroyed buildings which fell like snow. The Amis turned and flew away leaving behind them on the ground the tank and infantry battle to run its course.' To the east, in long rushes of movement covered by the fire of the panzers and of their own grenadier comrades, groups of ss men bombed and machine pistolled their way toward and into the Garcelles woods. Defending the area were riflemen of the lorried infantry component of 1st Polish Armoured Division. This was the Poles' first major battle, but even before they had come into action they had lost eight killed and twenty-eight wounded when their columns had been bombed, in error, by the us Air Force attacking Falaise. The sufferings of the Poles were not to end there. At Cramesnil in the early afternoon of 8 August, the first squadrons of 2nd Armoured Regiment came under fire as the Stuart tanks approached the minor road from Cintheaux to St Sylvain. From the hedges along the road teams of ss men armed with Panzerfaust and Panzerschreck waited patiently while behind them the anti-tank guns opened up at maximum range and destroyed the tanks of the first wave. The Polish line halted; within the range of the rocket launchers. There were streams of flame, pale in the hot sunshine, as the grenadiers launched their missiles and then came the noise of explosions. The Polish tanks began to burn. Machine guns opened up upon the tank crews racing for cover and upon the infantry moving forward to support the armoured vehicles. Petrol from the burning tanks had ignited the corn through which they had been moving and acrid blue smoke rose and hung motionless in the still air. Through the smoke advanced the leading troops of the Polish second wave and these, too, were destroyed. The 2nd Squadron moved forward and into range. The ss opened fire again and the wireless waves were full of alarmed reports as first one, then three and finally the whole first line of the 2nd Squadron was attacked and ruined. The ss Pak, the Panzerfaust teams and the Panthers had fought a very successful defensive battle. On the flank the Polish 24th Lancers too had suffered a beating and had been unable to give drive to the attack by 51st Highland Division; Operation Totalize was already beginning to run out of steam as losses mounted; from the 1st and 2nd Squadrons of the Polish Armoured Regiment for example twenty-six from a total of thirty-six tanks committed to battle had been destroyed. At one point no fewer than nine Shermans were destroyed by a single 8.8 cm gun.

In the woods of Garcelles the Polish riflemen were up against a determined and ruthless enemy. Despite their rawness the Poles fought hard but against the young German veterans they were outclassed. Their resistance was beaten down and the ss advance swung through the thick, dark woods. Wittmann's Tigers, meanwhile, had engaged the Allied armour and the long-barrelled 8.8 cm cannon were destroying the Shermans and Stuarts of the 4th Canadian Armoured Division at distances which their armament could not meet. The Canadians and the Poles were in confusion; the aim of the German pre-emptive attack had succeeded and Wittmann's tanks moved back to Cintheaux and there collaborated with the defenders to drive back another Allied attack coming down from the north. Perhaps attack is too strong a term

107

to describe the Canadian operations. They were more like determined probes and each was held, deflected or turned back. Along the whole ss battle line the fighting rose and fell in intensity. From Garcelles to the Cramesnil woods at St Sylvain the noise of battle rolled as the grenadiers of the Hitler Youth Division, supported by the remnants of Wünsche's panzer regiment, fought the Canadian and Polish infantry and armour. At last light there was a reduction of pressure and both sides took stock of the situation and regrouped. The Canadians brought up replacements and reinforcements ready to begin the assault at dawn for already their time-table was not running true. This delay to their advance was due in great part to the timely arrival upon the battlefield of part of Wünsche's regiment and the Panther battalion commanded by Jurgensen, whose attacks had stopped 'Operation Totalize' dead in its tracks.

On the left flank of the ss was the hamlet of Bretteville-sur-Laize still held by a remnant of 89th Division and toward and against this forlorn hope flooded the infantry waves of 2nd Canadian Division. The Canadians pressed forward over the trenches in which the German infantry had stayed to the last until the leading troops had penetrated so far that the left flank of the Waldmuller battle group had been turned. Forced to give way under this pressure the ss moved back in the night to the line of the Laison which they were then ordered to hold until 85th Division, marching hot-foot from the Seine, arrived to relieve them. The grenadiers regrouped and took up the new positions. Waldmuller detachment was sent to dig in on a sector which extended from Point 140 to Point 183, along the Caen–Falaise road, while the Krause group took position on the heights to the north of Maizières and Rouvres. The remnants of Obloeter's 3rd Battalion detachment in the Krause group went to Point 195 and put out a cachment line to halt, assemble and to bring back into the firing line the elements of 89th Division which had been scattered and dispersed by the day's fighting. The divisional headquarters defence company went back into reserve and Wünsche's panzers took up position in the Quesnay woods.

The collapse of 89th Division produced a crisis in the Command of 7th Army and led to an exchange of telephone calls between the Supreme Commander in the West, von Kluge, and the commander of 5th Panzer Army, General Dietrich. Kluge, still very new to conditions in Normandy, promised to send to the Falaise sector the tanks of 9th ss Panzer Division which were being held for use against the Americans in the Argentan area but during the course of these conversations it became clear that what was being discussed was not a regiment of tanks but only a dozen vehicles, all of which were involved in fighting on another sector. The 2nd ss Panzer Corps to which 9th ss belonged was ordered to release some of its armour and to send it post haste to Falaise. The ss Heavy Tank Battalion 102, with a total of 13 machines under command out of the 45 which had begun the campaign, was selected.

This independent tank battalion had been raised in the spring of 1944, and after D-Day had acted as a fire brigade unit being rushed from one threatened spot to another; here to seal off an Allied penetration, there to lead an advance temporarily halted. Now it was heading northwards to support the crumbling front, for news had been received at 07.00 hrs on the morning of 9 August that a fresh Allied penetration had been made. No. 2 Company, at instant readiness, moved out from Chênedollé and went via Condé to the western side of Falaise to support 271st Division, holding the line from St Germain to Cossesseville. The vehicles of Nos. 1 and 3 Companies secured the Falaise road.

During the night of 8/9 August a fresh crisis situation developed. It will be remembered that the Waldmuller group had set out to reach an area between Points 140 and 183. The Canadians, meanwhile, in an attempt to wrest from the ss the initiative which had been lost had sent forward 4th Armoured Brigade, to take Point 105. But this unit had lost its bearings and by error had ascended the slopes of Point 140, had occupied the crest without opposition and before the Waldmuller group had reached it. When that unit arrived it was met with tank and machine gun fire from the British Columbia and the Algonquin Regiments which had consolidated upon the crest. The Waldmuller group was deflected eastwards and was cut off from the main body of the Division. The grenadiers spent long hours waiting for the onset of darkness under cover of which they intended to strike for the German lines. A similar fate had befallen the Defence Company which had been overtaken, attacked and dispersed by the Poles, en route to the divisional reserve area near Potigny.

It was of paramount importance that the Canadians be ejected from Point 140. It was one of the highest points in the immediate area and commanded the Laison river. From its peak there was complete observation across the whole of the ground to the south and south east and it was through that area that 85th Division would have to pass on its way to relieve the Hitler Youth from the line. An armoured pincer movement was planned to drive the Canadians from the hill. From the west the Tigers of 501st Battalion were to drive in to open the attack and then from the east would come Jurgensen's Panthers. At the sound of the Maybach engines the Canadians knew that an attack upon them was imminent and that they were isolated and out of touch with their own main body. The Shermans deployed and chose their ground opening fire upon the Tigers rumbling out of the small wood which crowns the northern and western slopes of the hill. The Tigers moved into dead ground under which cover they worked their way forward until they could open fire with the deadliest effect upon the Canadian tanks. Within seconds two machines had been destroyed and then the Tigers roared out on to the open slopes of the hill firing their cannon with such accuracy that in tank versus tank battles five more Shermans were destroyed. A Polish infantryman described how he observed the battle and saw black clouds rise in the air as the German tank guns 'brewed up' one Canadian tank after another. Cloud after cloud rose into the hot summer sky, each of them telling of the destruction of the British Columbia Regiment's tanks. The Tigers had had no loss and then as the Allied force teetered on the edge of indecision, whether to stand and fight on to total destruction or to void the battle-field, from behind them and passing the copse of birch trees on the lower slopes of the hill came the Panthers. Quickly they gained the crest and joined the battle. Forty-seven Canadian machines were destroyed and 116 men lost during that short engagement.

There was no lull after the first bitter battle and the ss panzers and grenadiers had to spend much of the rest of the day fighting down the resistance of the small detachments of the Canadians who still held out. Into the battle came the bicycle-mounted companies of 85th Division and the arrival of these fresh troops enabled the Canadians to be driven headlong from the crest and down the slopes. Then came the time to regroup the survivors of the ss battle squads and to count the cost of the operations. Of all the losses which had been suffered in the fighting of the past two days none was felt more deeply than that of Michael Wittmann who fell in action on 8 August. During the battle at Cintheaux he had attacked a group of Sherman tanks head on and had smashed two of them. The remaining five opened fire upon him and at point blank range. No crew members were seen to leave the Tiger. Wittmann, who had destroyed 138 tanks and self-propelled guns, had put out of action no fewer than 132 anti-tank guns, the most successful tank fighter of the Second World War, had fallen.

Both the Krause and the Waldmuller battle groups had been reduced by losses and had each only the strength of a weak grenadier company. The ss men, worn out by the strain of weeks of unending combat, sank to the ground and slept where they fell. They were totally exhausted but once again they were aroused from their leaden sleep and called to action. Against Point 195 which the British Columbia Regiment had failed to attack, a thorough assault was now made. Behind a furious bombardment the Argyll and Sutherland Highlanders of Canada advanced and struck at the weak Grenadier line. Crack troops from the Dominion met the élite Grenadiers of the Hitler Youth and the fighting in the darkness was often hand to hand with bayonet, knife or entrenching tool as the Scots battled their way forward. Violet-coloured flares from the grenadier trenches rose into the night sky and in reply to this call for help the few remaining panzers rolled forward firing to such effect that the Argyll advance was halted and then driven back. As the Scots withdrew they were bombarded from the front by the panzers on the ridge and then taken in flank by Wünsche's armour concealed in the Quesnay woods. Under this double punch the Canadian infantry flooded back to its old line.

On the left flank of the Canadians, where 1st Polish Armoured Division held post, there had also been heavy fighting throughout the night of 8/9 August. Against the flank of the Waldmuller group 1st Polish Armoured Regiment had initially been sent in to break through and to support the Canadians on Point 140, but this attack was aborted and new assaults were ordered. The objective now was Soignolles.

As the Polish squadrons debouched from the woods in which they had been concealed their first line was met with fire from giant rocket propelled mortars whose projectiles set fire to the wheat standing yellow and ready for harvesting. As the tanks emerged from the acrid blue smoke screen they came under fire from panzers and from anti-tank guns hidden in the hedges and copses lining a road to the right of the axis of advance and others set upon high ground. The German fire halted the Polish line as first one and then a second machine was hit and destroyed; then a third stopped, its track blown off by a mine. A fourth was hit in the turret and backed into the smoke, its main armament destroyed by shell fire. Baulked by the ss gunnery the Poles extended their left wing, seeking a way round the flank of the determined troops ahead of them. At last light the Poles went in again and thrust past Soignolles heading for Point 111, a slight hill on the Maizières road and east of Point 140. Their advance crossed the front of the German anti-tank line and they entered a corridor of weapons handled by men determined to resist rather than surrender. The night of 9 August was full of sound and colour: the crash of explosions, the sound of steel striking steel, the showers of sparks in the darkness as armour piercing shot struck the Shermans' armour plate, the trails of fire from the Panzerfaust, green flares from the German front line trenches and the slow red curve of tracer in the night. Under the ss fire the Poles were forced back and withdrew to their concentration area. Behind them in the corn fields across which they tried to advance lay thirteen of their tanks destroyed or burning. The defence of the northern sector was holding firm.

The armour had failed; now it was the turn of the Polish infantry to force the line. Small parties of riflemen, some with tank support, tried to infiltrate through the dark woods and past the Krause group, heading eastwards and trying to force a crossing of the Laison river at Condé. To hold the open flank of that sector the battle group commander had been able to spare only a single anti-tank gun but this fired upon the Polish armour to such effect that within a short time nine vehicles had been destroyed. Just east of the Falaise road a second Polish assault by 3rd Brigade was put in at Estrées-la-Campagne and Point 111, the hill which had cost 1st Armoured Regiment so many casualties. These were to be night attacks and the first assaults were driven back by machine gun and mortar fire. The whole front was alive. The night sky was coloured with fires from villages burning on both sides of the line, the brief flare of explosions and the slow burning of tanks and lorries. The Polish assault flooded forward again up to the edge of the ss trenches and for a second time was driven back. It was early morning and although the fighting had abated it had not died away for patrols met each other in the darkness and battles among small groups and even individual soldiers went on all night. The ss were obeying their commander's orders and were holding fast. Then at first light 9th Polish Infantry Battalion made yet another attempt upon Point 111 and this succeeded. A small breach had been made in the German line.

Back with the Krause group the single anti-tank gun had long since been silent. Its crew was dead, killed by the concentrated fire of the surviving tanks of the Polish squadron. In front of the Polish armour lay a gap in the ss line open for them to exploit but, inexplicably, they did not press forward but instead withdrew northwards. The Poles were making a gallant effort and their probing attacks broke through the ss front at many places. At one point a local breach was rapidly exploited by a Polish tank and armoured infantry group but unfortunately for the Poles they were on a collision course with a vedette of ss panzer and a self-propelled detachment which had joined forces and were heading northwards to close the reported gap in the line. The German 7.5 cm guns opened up on the Poles at close range and their advance which had flooded forward with such confidence was driven back with a loss of forty of their machines.

The arrival of 85th Division in the line on 10 August enabled 12th ss Division's sector to be handed over. Like 12th ss the 85th Infantry was a new division, raised only during the spring of 1944. The infantry was formed into two grenadier regiments, the 1054th and 1055th, but these were the only units up to strength. When the 85th Division moved forward to the battle zone it had only seventy-five per cent of its requirements in light weapons and automatics; there were insufficient horses to draw the artillery pieces and a serious shortage of lorries and motor vehicles.

The fighting troops of 85th Division had crossed the Seine on 7 August and were eventually posted to the ss Panzer Corps in the Falaise area where their first active service duty was to take over from the Hitler Youth on the heights north west of the Laison river with the task of halting an enemy break-through towards Falaise. By the early hours of the 9th the advance guard of 1055th Regiment had reached its allotted area but the rest of the Division could not be brought forward.

The Army High Command had ordered that we maintain wireless silence so that the British would not realize that the fought-out 12th ss had been relieved. There was no contact with the other components of Division by wireless and we were forced to rely upon motor cycle despatch riders who were unfamiliar with the country. The units had all suffered from air attacks. We had had to march a great part of the way on paths parallel to the road and this cross-country marching was very tiring. We were worn out and could not have relieved our ss comrades in that condition. They agreed to hold the line for another day.

When the Division did move forward to take over the sector was quiet and it was hoped that the officers would have time to familiarize themselves with their positions, but Canadian silent infiltration tactics had brought up Allied soldiers between the 85th's regiments and the ss positions they were to occupy. The men of that division had to fight their way forward to reach the ss lines and on the right flank had to mount a full-scale attack to force back a Canadian armoured reconnaissance group which had penetrated the line to the north of La Bû-sur-Rouvres.

There was a growing strength in the probes and patrols which the Canadians and Poles sent out which left no doubt that the Allies would once again attempt the break-through to seize Falaise. The remainder of the 85th Division had by now come into the line and the fighting troops were ready for action.

The 12th ss, meanwhile, had taken up reserve positions along a sector between Evreux and Bernay where they rested and regrouped. Roll calls showed their crippling losses and the strength return on 13 August illustrated that the Division, which had gone into action on 7 June with a strength of over 18,000 men, had been reduced within two months to a strength of only 500. Only twenty of the divisional panzers were 'runners'. One battery of 8.8 cm guns, a heavy howitzer battery and one of 15 cm cannon, together with nine self-propelled guns of 3.7 cm calibre were the only artillery support. These divisional remnants were combined into a single battle group.

It was during this time that the possibility of the Allies pocketing the German armies became a realizable proposition. The American and French advances along the southern flank towards Argentan and Alençon, the eastern side-stepping of the Poles on the northern flank who were trying to edge round the ss resistance, and the delay in withdrawing the most westerly German groups, had begun to shape the pocket. Dietrich, GOC of 5th Panzer Army, was not alone in voicing his fears of encirclement but no heed was taken of these warnings given by the men on the spot. The Allies, aware now of the strategic possibilities that could be theirs, concentrated on driving eastwards to fling an iron ring around the Germans and to enclose them tightly. Operation Tractable, the follow-up to the dying Operation Totalize, might have been designed for exactly the type of interdiction which was necessary, for its stated aim was to deny the use of the roads through Falaise to the German armies.

About 10 km east of Falaise flowed the river Dives. Its widest extent in that sector was only 10 m but its banks were steep and an obstacle to traffic. Crossings would, therefore, be restricted to fords and bridges, but these were few in number and the roads and tracks leading to those points were of poor quality and quite unsuitable for the continual passage of the heavy military vehicles which would use them. The loss by the Germans of any crossing point on the Dives would reduce the avenues of future escape. Their failure to control any road would restrict the passage of the armies. The capture by the Allies of any nodal point would be a matter of such concern that instant heavy and, where necessary, repeated counter-attacks would be launched, regardless of loss, to regain them. On the northern flank the town of Falaise had now taken on a critical importance and in descending order of military priority were the towns and villages which controlled the crossings across the Dives; Trun, St Pierre-sur-Dives, Jort, Morteaux-Coliboeuf, Chambois and St Lambert-sur-Dives.

Field Marshal von Kluge had become aware of the danger of encirclement and realized it was time for the 7th Army and for 5th Panzer Army to begin its withdrawal. But in the mind of the Führer gnawed still the belief that a renewal of the offensive to Avranches would succeed. To him the equation was still valid that a metre of Norman soil was of more importance than 10 km of ground in any other part of France. No. 2 Company of the Tiger Battalion had taken up position on the left flank facing the British bridgehead at Thury Harcourt and during 9 and 10 August had been in support of 271st Division. Within hours of the Company's arrival it had gone into action to fight back an Allied tanks' thrust near the Grimbosq woods and in the course of this one junior commander destroyed four British tanks and by his action compelled the remaining British armour to withdraw.

Panzermeyer, aware of how weak were the German units in his command, carried out a reconnaissance to fix a new defence line which his division was to take up in their support of the 85th Division. This ran from Point 159 to the Dives river and, because of shortage of infantry, could not be continuous but would be a series of strong points extending along the ridge. The divisional orders to the Grenadiers were stark and simple: this line would be held to the last. It ran along the hills above the valley of the Ainte river, a tributary of the Dives, and thus controlled the road which descended towards Trun, a main route eastwards out of the encirclement and one along which were already marching columns of infantry, batteries of horse artillery, soft skin and armoured vehicles all heading in the direction of the river Vie.

> Until that time we did not know that the forces in Normandy were in such a serious situation. I do not think that any of us was aware that a pocket had been created and that we were inside it. We held our positions and concentrated upon the battle in hand; after all as infantry our view was restricted to what was happening within our own company or battalion area. By the Monday when the line moved back and we were passed on the road by convoys heading towards the Seine, then we guessed that we would have to do a rear-guard action.

On the Thury-Harcourt sector during the early morning of 12 August, twenty-six Allied tanks struck at and broke through the German battle line east of Barbéry and No. 2 Tiger Company went in to seal off this penetration. Leaving one Panzer VI to guard the Espine road and a second to protect the flank facing Fresnay, the remaining six armoured fighting vehicles rolled along the Barbéry road, reached the high ground along the northern edge of a wood and then swung into the attack. At long range the Tigers opened fire and there followed a short, intense tank duel during which seven Allied tanks and an armoured car were destroyed. But during the fighting Allied tanks worked their way forward and in the close quarter battle one Tiger was hit and 'brewed up'. Although the loss of just that one machine represented a serious reduction in German strength the Tiger attack had restored the situation and the battle line was sealed. The Allied tanks withdrew and a penetration heading south eastwards towards Falaise had been halted. On 12 August von Kluge, who had at last received authorization to withdraw from Mortain, began the eastward movement of 7th and 5th Panzer Armies. Mortain fell to the US forces and on the north-western front the Canadian Corps and British 12th Corps had gained touch.

The Canadian Command was determined to renew the assault and to prepare for this resumption of the offensive opened up, during the afternoon, a long and intensive barrage upon the sector in which they planned to make their break-through. Then a smoke screen was laid by bombardment and under cover of this the Canadian armour came on again. Once again a single Tiger guarding the northern flank destroyed five of the leading squadrons in quick and easy succession. The other Canadian vehicles backed into the smoke and as they moved away German grenadiers swung forward in a counter-attack to regain the ground which had been lost. With their task fulfilled and the Sherman thrust destroyed, the Tigers of Nos. 1 and 3 Companies withdrew into reserve near Château de la Motte. The No. 2 Tiger Company had also had a hard day's fighting during which it had put out of action eleven tanks and a lorry but its own strength had been reduced by losses and at last light it had only four panzers still ready for action.

The 13th of August passed without incident on 85th Division's sector except for an incursion by Allied tanks near La Bû-sur-Rouvres.

The 272nd Division held post on the right flank of 85th Division and during this anxious time had fought only local engagements. Pressure upon the 1st SS Corps front had tended to concentrate itself along the Falaise road and the sights and sounds indicated that a resumption of the Allied offensive would not be long delayed and would be made on that sector. This new Operation, Tractable, was launched on Monday 14 August, but on the evening of the 13th a complete set of plans were found on the body of a dead Canadian officer and armed with this information the SS front line was withdrawn so that it was upon vacated trenches and empty strong points that the bombs of the Allied air forces fell. The 85th Division was not so fortunate and on its front the mass bombing broke a breach in the line through which roared an armoured phalanx supported by infantry of 3rd Canadian Division. But the Canadians did not use their armour as aggressively as the opportunities demanded and restricted it to the role of infantry support. The strategic potential was wasted in short limited advances. Nevertheless the Canadians slowly made ground until they had reached and crossed the Falaise–St Pierre-sur-Dives road. They pressed the advance forward towards Falaise but at a point some 5 km north of the town a remnant of ss grenadiers was rushed into battle and this small group held the threatened break-through.

On the left of the Canadians the dawn mist of 14 August had been thickened by smoke shells under cover of which screen the Canadian infantry attacked and their advances turned the Grenadier flank. Shermans moved forward to exploit the situation and opened fire upon the Tigers, halted and in position. During this exchange of fire Allied infantry had come up and their presence threatened the German armour. The Tigers, in an attempt to dominate a situation which threatened to deteriorate rapidly, drove about the cornfields and hedgerows apparently not noticing that Canadian anti-tank guns and greater amounts of armour had moved forward. Fire was opened at close range upon three of the German vehicles, but the Tiger at close range was even more lethal than at long range and within seconds two Shermans were smashed. So destructive was the impact of one shell from the long-barelled 8.8 cm gun that the Sherman turret was flung high into the air and slowly cartwheeled, over and over. A salvo of shells hit a Panzer VI and it burnt so fiercely and so quickly that the crew did not escape. German grenadiers moved forward to restore the line and to protect the Tigers from the attentions of the Canadian infantry and under this grenadier pressure the Canadian infantry were pushed back. Then the German advance was itself stopped short as more Canadian armour moved forward and it seemed as if the ground for which the Grenadiers had fought so hard would be lost again. Then a Tiger rolled on to the battle-field fresh from the repair workshops only a kilometre away, and bolstered by this support the Canadians were flung back. Jurgensen's Panthers which had been guarding the flank were then able to withdraw and as they moved the Allied air forces began to bomb Potigny. The Panzer Company and the Grenadier Company, now reduced to only ten men, started to withdraw under the rain of bombs but were halted and ordered to occupy and to hold Point 183, north of Potigny. Their advance to capture this upland opened at 18.30 hrs and reached the wooded area 1 km east of Souligny but as the tired grenadiers began to dig their foxholes in the hard and stony sun-baked earth of Normandy through their line flooded German infantry hotly pursued by twelve Shermans. The grenadiers stood to and opened fire with panzerfaust upon the armoured vehicles. Three more Canadian vehicles were knocked out to make a total of fourteen destroyed that day. But the Germans, too, had suffered losses and both 1st and 3rd Tiger Companies had been savagely reduced in number and the No. 2 Company had only three 'runners'. The workshop companies repaired the damaged Tigers within firing distance of the battle-field but Canadian pressure made it likely that the workshops would be overrun by the Allied advance. Difficulties with the lorries bringing forward the spares and petrol to the forward units played their part in reducing the tank strength. The congestion on the roads, the limited access to the pocket and the constantly changing battle positions meant that many lorries could not find their parent units which then went unprovided for.

Along the whole of the northern flank of the pocket hard and bitter fighting went on throughout the day and in the ranks of the ss there grew the conviction that they were holding open the door through which their comrades were able to escape eastwards. The British spearheads in the north were only 18 km from those in the south belonging to the French who were now the most westerly unit on the southern flank. The escape corridor was narrowing, was already congested and, therefore, a prime target for the Allied fighter bombers which swept down and along the whole length of the bottleneck rocket-bombing the convoys moving slowly out of the encirclement. The troops holding the walls along the corridor of escape were under the most severe pressure and their difficulties were heightened, in the sector held by 85th Division, when the ss artillery which had supported it was removed and sent to the sensitive left wing. On the right flank which was coming increasingly under pressure the 85th was to be forced to rely upon the support of its own understrength artillery battalions as well as that of a few weak detachments from Corps artillery and the Luftwaffe flak. The increasing difficulties in ammunition supply and the failure of limbers to arrive through the press of vehicles, which were heading east, added to the frustration which was felt in not being able to reply to the rolling and crushing Allied barrages.

In the middle morning of 14 August Canadian left wing infantry supported by nearly 500 tanks advanced behind a thundering barrage and covered by fighter bomber attacks of the RAF. The Canadian tank waves crushed what little opposition the German could put up and the armoured spearheads went via Ifs-sur-Laison and Ernes across the Laison river, rolling up the divisional front, overrunning the grenadier companies and breaking through to Maizières and Rouvres. Unable to limber up and to withdraw their pieces from the battlefield the gunners of the 85th's artillery fired over open sights at the Canadian tanks as they roared forward. Tanks, singly and in twos, began to halt or to burn as the gunners shot off the last of the ammunition as fast as they could load. The outcome was inevitable for the number of tanks exceeded the density of the gun line and soon the 8.8 cm and the smaller anti-tank guns lay silent and broken in the wheat fields, but on the heights south east of Maizières and Quilly-le-Tesson more than forty of the Canadian tanks lay ruined. The Allied thrust tore the villages of Sassy and Olendon from German hands by mid-afternoon and then struck eastwards and southwards, towards the Dives river and the village of Trun, moving across the front of the ss units, pushing back 85th Division and outflanking Falaise. Another virile thrust would take , the Canadian Corps across the major escape route of the Vendeuvre road.

The Canadian advance began to fan out, the 85th Division's Fusilier Battalion and two Engineer companies, the last reserve, were flung in and by hand to hand fighting halted the Canadian advance on the heights to the south east of Sassy and Olendon. The divisional front was disintegrating and with it the whole of the northern flank. On the right wing in the area of the great woods north of Vendeuvre there was only the loosest contact with 272nd Division. On the left, along the Caen–Falaise road, the 1054th Regiment was fighting together with close combat artillery, an anti-tank company and a group of panzers from 12th ss Division against determined drives by the Canadians and the Polish 8th Infantry Battalion which was attacking in the Quesnay woods. On 85th Division's extreme left was 89th Division with which there was no connection at all.

On the main ss front to the north of Falaise there was, during the afternoon of the 15th, another determined drive by the Canadians to seize Potigny, only 6 km north of the town and soon 102nd Panzer Battalion was fighting for its life. Allied artillery poured down a heavy concentration of smoke shells under cover of which a heavily reinforced tank and infantry group crashed through. Throughout the long, hot afternoon the Tigers fired round after round at the advancing armada of armour. A Tiger was hit at 19.00 hrs and burst into flames. Now only a few remained and in the darkness of the night of 15 August this battered group withdrew to the northern suburbs of Falaise.

Along the rest of Corps front the battle to hold back the Allied drive was bitter and fierce but the strongest efforts of the divisions could not disguise the fact that the High Command had made the most grievous errors. The 85th Division, for example, had been sent in against a highly mechanized army without the heavy anti-tank guns and the self-propelled artillery which were essential for it to survive in combat, and within a space of six hours 85th Division had lost the mass of its infantry and artillery and, thus, its main fighting strength. During the night of the 14th/15th a new but weak line was formed on the heights hard by the Dives river between Vendeuvre and Bernières d'Ailly and on the northwestern edge of the forest on Les Monts d'Erames north west of Morteaux–Coliboeuf. Every kind of splinter group or fragment of a military formation which could be scraped together was assembled to hold the front, including a company of half-trained recruits from 185th Battalion. By such experiences the line was manned and by the energetic efforts of the senior officers contact was restored between the units within the Division and the formations on its flanks.

The military situation for both sides was that a definite pocket had been formed within which were concentrated the bulk of two German armies, 7th and 5th Panzer. The farther east the Allies drove the longer the pocket became and it was a race between the Allies, who hoped to extend and increase the encirclement, and the Germans intending by swift evacuation to empty their troops out of the trap.

On the German side attempts were now being made to establish a line which was to be held literally until the last man. To bolster that line and to give it strength artillery was taken from every unit which could spare it and from many which could not. One such was 85th Division and from the artillery units supporting that formation the High Command ordered, during the night of 14th/15th, the withdrawal of all the Luftwaffe flak units. With them went the last hope of the hard-pressed infantry battalions to fight a battle with any hope of success. Together with those batteries went also a flak battalion which had been guarding against aerial assault the vital crossings of the Dives on both sides of Jort.

Simonds, the Canadian Corps Commander, now realized that the town of Falaise was no longer the objective and that the emphasis had moved further eastwards to the banks of the Dives. It was on that river that the fate of the trapped Germans would be decided and in order to give greater power to his left wing he swung towards Jort and the river the 4th Canadian and 1st Polish Armoured divisions. Their task was to strike eastwards as rapidly as possible, and then to drive southwards down the bank of the river to join with the French and the Americans striking northwards to the nodal point of Trun.

The Polish move began on the hot morning of 15 August and having crossed at right angles the rear details of three Allied divisions still striking southwards towards Falaise they drove across the gently rolling and open countryside between Sassy and Jort and descended towards the village of Vendeuvre which lies in the valley of the Dives. Along the northern side of the Maizières–Vendeuvre road lay a long and narrow piece of woodland and along the Sassy–Vendeuvre road a smaller, squarer piece of forest behind which lay the railway station, the river and then some more woodland. The Polish tanks advancing to capture Vendeuvre before going on to Trun were thus entering a trap bounded on three sides by anti-tank guns and bazooka teams. As the Mounted Rifles leading the Polish advance moved down the gentle slope German anti-tank guns opened up from the tree line and Tiger tanks, moving about on the right flank near the Falaise–Jort road, also opened fire. The Polish tanks halted and observed the ground before them. There was the long straggling village dominated by the church. The Dives river formed two streams just below Jort and some miles behind that place the forest of Montpinçon rose dark on the horizon.

Fresh reports came in of panzer movement on the flank and a squadron turned to face the challenge. Other tanks took the German anti-tank guns under fire and soon a battle was in full progress. Within minutes the PAK had smashed two of the Polish machines but then the remaining tanks concentrated their fire and had soon knocked out the German weapons. The squadrons continued to advance via the village station to find a ford across the river. During the advance there were more losses: two tanks were hit and immobilized and another two suffered broken tracks from the torn-up ground. Only nine machines were left from the squadrons and slowly the remnants moved up and down the river banks looking for a shallow place. A driver accelerated, mud spurted, water splashed high in the air as the machine churned its way across the river bed and struggled to ascend the bank. The Poles had crossed the Dives.

While one group was forcing the river line other machines had opened fire upon the Tigers who had, at last, come to battle. Five Polish tanks were lost in the fierce little fight, two burnt out and three severely damaged, and one Tiger had been destroyed. A third squadron was ordered forward to enter Vendeuvre and fought down bazooka teams and machine gunners, thrusting onwards to seize the bridge, too late, for this was blown by the German rear-guard. Further advance was impossible for the banks of the river in the centre of the village were unscaleable to tanks. The Polish squadrons, having defeated the Germans at Vendeuvre, swung their guns towards Jort and brought the village under fire, their shells falling upon the German cars and waggons passing through the streets and out of the pocket.

Although the orders to withdraw from the pocket had still not been issued and, indeed, plans to resume the western advance had still not been abandoned, the exits from the pocket were packed with traffic. For once the terrible German efficiency had failed and its failure condemned many to death or captivity. There were no bridges built across the rivers, no crossing places reconnoitred, no axis of advance kept open to nourish the troops in the pocket and none left open for those units whose slow pace would retard the flow of the fast formations. All roads leading eastwards were jammed with cars, lorries, tanks and carts wheel to wheel and bumper to bumper. The pace was slow and the halts long as lorries, overburdened and lacking proper service and maintenance, broke down on the narrow country roads jamming the road back for miles at a time. Messengers, despatch riders, ambulances and supplies – all the essential needs of war – were held up. One person to whom the choked roads were to spell disgrace and death was von Kluge, the Supreme Commander in the West. His offensive at Mortain had failed and Hitler had insisted that it had failed because Kluge had wanted it not to succeed. Obsessed, as he was, by thoughts that others were betraying him Hitler refused to believe that von Kluge had been caught in a monster traffic jam and had, therefore, been unable to contact his headquarters. To Hitler his silence was a sign of treachery. Von Kluge was removed from office and poisoned himself on the way back to Germany.

Above the wide, slow moving columns swooped and roared the aircraft of the Allies, bombing and machine gunning at will, opposed in most cases only by the rifle fire that exasperated soldiers opened up upon them as they fled into the open fields to avoid the rockets, bombs and machine gun bullets which were sprayed and fired at them. The Typhoons circled in the cloudless skies above the pocket of death, waiting their turn to descend upon the close-packed mass and to cause new fires, fresh casualties and greater consternation with their low level passes above the cowering heads of the groups of men gathered in the roads and paths. Already the trees and hedges in the area were a mess of torn branches and leafless stumps, littering the cratered broken ground among the dead and dying men. The smells were of fires, rubber burning, blood, the heavy urine smell of horse sweat, and of the dead, men and cattle. The whole area was a galimaufrey of sounds and smells, which turned the stomach with their bitterness and tore the heart with their tragedy.

Although Vendeuvre, Jort and Bernières d'Ailly fell to the Allied thrusts on the sector held by Panzermeyer's grenadiers each and every Canadian attempt was driven back. Point 159 was a corner-stone of the ss defensive line and had been the object of a number of heavy and persistent Canadian assaults. Against this feature, lying slightly to the north of the Falaise–Jort road and thus obstructing lateral movement by the Canadian forces, the Allied attacks came in, usually behind heavy and long bombardments and often with bombing and strafing attacks by the Typhoons and Spitfires. 'When we looked south or south-eastwards and could see a road the traffic on it seemed never to move. We could tell where the road ran even if we could not see it for above it all day long flew the Allied aircraft. It seemed odd that the Allies could have so many machines. So many that they could attack the road and still have aeroplanes over to bomb us.' On the 85th Division's front the pressure of the Polish and Canadian armour slowly forced southwards the men of 1054th regiment, gaining ground throughout the midday and afternoon's baking heat until Perrières and Epancy had both been lost. Without pause the Allied advance drove back the army units and the ss were forced to conform by withdrawing behind the Falaise–Jort road and moving towards the heavily forested uplands of Les Monts d'Erames. There the advance was halted, brought to a stop by fanatical resistance. The fighting was desperate; this high ground was one of the few dominant features still in German hands and if the pocket was to be held then the upper ground had to be held – and firmly held. The Canadian–Polish forces strove hard to drive back the men of 85th Division from their positions; barrage followed barrage, assault followed assault and still the soldiers held the break-through to the south. During one of the more furious passages of artillery fire a salvo of shells destroyed the last remaining anti-tank gun on 85th Division's sector leaving the infantry regiments defenceless against the Canadian armour which now began to pour forward. On the eastern flank of the Division at Jort there had also been a break-through. The final pair of 8.8 cm guns sited behind the church and dominating the bridges across the two riverlets had opened fire upon the

121

Stuarts and Cromwells driving through the narrow streets and caused casualties. The Polish armour was forced to accept the punishment until a troop of tanks crossed the bridges, fanned out and began to fire upon the guns which had tormented them. High explosive shells began to fall around the guns but still the crews continued to load and to fire at the Polish tanks now to the front of them and moving round the flank. Within minutes the 88s were silenced and the way ahead up the gentle slope to Courcy and to a wider encirclement of the pocket lay within the Polish grasp. The Cromwells halted to consolidate their position and waited, and while they were immobile splinter groups of the German infantry formed a thin defence line. More and more men filtered back through the Canadian lines to reach the divisional positions and reinforce a weak and desperately tired battle group which had the numerical strength of only two weak battalions.

With his infantry so completely exhausted the line could not be held and the divisional commander ordered that the remnants from the artillery groups be put into the line so as to give the infantry a short break from the continual battle.

I had never known such tiredness. It caused hallucinations and a complete sense of non-being. Back in the so-called rest area the cooks had prepared a meal but it was too much effort to eat it, hungry though we were. We craved for sleep and slept like the dead; we could have slept for days. Next morning was the worst. All the tensions came back, the tensions that one forgets in the line and I began remembering almost with nostalgia the long march to the Seine. How long ago it seemed and yet it had been less than two weeks away in time.

On the eastern flank the Canadians and Poles began to push along the valley of the Dives but their probes had little force and made little ground during the morning of the 16th. During the afternoon, however, their pressure increased and struck not only against the artillery/infantry of 85th Division but also the ss armoured reconnaissance detachment and five panzers which had been moved to the threatened flank. Once again recourse was made to patching and darning the holes in the line with scratch units but the line held even against this greater pressure. During the night the 85th's infantry regiments, now reduced to two battalions in strength, moved back into the line taking back the positions which had been held by the artillerymen.

To the east of the Dives the Poles were strongly established and had built bridges across the muddy river; the bridgehead was being extended, gaining ground slowly but steadily and the division was gathering its strength preparing itself for the next operation. This would be a continuation of the southward drive which would end at Chambois and where a link up would be made with the forces on the southern flank whereby a ring would have been thrown round the German armies. The last acts of the drama were about to be played in the fields of Normandy, and meanwhile on the southern Mediterranean coast of France Allied forces had begun to land in a second D-Day.

On the western sector of 1st ss Corps the grenadiers of the Hitler Youth were still battling to hold Point 159. Throughout the morning of Wednesday 16 August infantry attacks followed artillery barrages, trying to win the crest from the Hitler Youth. Towards midday a bombardment of unbelievable ferocity opened upon the ss positions around the hotly contested point. Through the smoke of the explosions and the clouds of dust raised by tank tracks drove the Shermans of the Regina Rifles roaring uphill in low gear towards the grenadiers situated on the torn-up high ground. The grenadiers had driven the supporting Canadian infantry to ground with volleys of well-directed machine gun fire and lacking the support of the foot the armour could not advance. The thrust halted at the foot of the hill and the Hitler Youth had, once again, stopped the tide of the Allied advance. The fighting, which lasted from 15 August and for much of 16 August, was marked by weak and unco-ordinated Canadian attacks which were usually driven back by the young ss veterans. As if seeking to open a way round the flank the fighter-bombers came in and struck at the Bois du Roi, to the left of Point 159 and on the western side of the Falaise–Caen road, in a diversionary attack and while the German attention was drawn away the Shermans made yet another and this time stronger assault upon Point 159. Their attritive tactics finally brought them victory and the hill, surrounded on three sides by Canadian infantry and armour, fell to their assault at midday on 16 August.

In the far west of the pocket the first moves had begun to withdraw from the western wall and by nightfall the troops on the north-western sector had been brought back to a point just east of Flers. The pocket was beginning to deflate and the offensive which had been begun to hem in the Americans had, within a week, been transmuted into a stalemate and then, within a further few days had gone on from an impasse to the destruction of much of the fighting strength of the two German armies.

During the succeeding days Allied pressure upon the flanks of 85th Division forced that formation farther and farther eastwards and the thrusting drive by 1st Polish Division by-passed its left flank. Indeed, by 17 August the 85th Division was no longer holding a cohesive front and was barely capable of offering determined resistance. The 12th ss Division was forced to take over a wider front embracing those sectors from which 85th Division had been driven. As the Allied pressure grew the 85th was forced even farther eastwards and northwards. Soon it was holding the ground between Montpinçon and Montviette and was no longer contained within the pocket. It now leaves this stage of the account.

Disintegration was now general and most units were fighting without central direction from divisional or Corps headquarters. Fragments of regiments and of battalions formed themselves into battle groups and fought on as self-contained units. To the Supreme Command and to the Supreme Commander in far-away East Prussia the flags on the maps seemed to indicate that the pocket was held by divisions and these were expected to hold divisional fronts and carry out divisional tasks even though, in most cases, their strength was reduced to single battalions of infantry, weak troops of panzer or shot-out batteries. So great was the disorder, the compression and the congestion within the confines of the pocket that most units ceased to record the passage of ordinary events in war diaries and concentrated upon only the most basic and essential information. 'One could not write a battalion war diary about the deeds of ten men in half a dozen holes on a sector half a kilometre wide', and thus the accounts of many brave men in those dying days have gone unrecorded and unrewarded.

Back on the Falaise sector the pressure by Canadian tank forces had driven the ss back across the Caen–Falaise highway and had begun to crack at long last the resistance put up by the ss. Despite the bolstering of this crumbling front by the Tigers of 102nd Battalion the Canadian thrust continued until, with the fall of Point 159, a gap had been forced into the Hitler Youth defences. Along the valley poured the Canadian armour, swung away from the waiting Tigers and pressed on and into Falaise which was garrisoned by the Hitler Youth. On Wednesday 16 August the Canadian leading troops entered the town which had been bombed in heavy attacks on 12–13 August and which had suffered such damage that whole streets had been obliterated. The attempt to interdict the east–west passage of the Germans by aerial bombing now inhibited the advance of the Canadian troops. Meanwhile the ss snipers and panzerfaust teams hidden in the rubble of the ruined houses took a heavy toll of them as they pushed southwards. There was bitter fighting and some of it for individual houses of tactical importance. Canadian pressure gradually eliminated the scattered pockets of resistance but then towards noon the last available Tigers were ordered into the town to support the hard-pressed grenadiers. They moved forward into the area of the cathedral and together with the infantry formed in that part of the city an immovable defence, standing firm while on either flank the Canadian advance drove slowly but steadily forward. Towards evening, with the full and certain knowledge that they had contributed to the defence of the town the Tigers withdrew to the south-western corner of the town. Fighting went on throughout the night of 16–17 August but nowhere in that town more fiercely than around the Ecole Supérieure in which sixty grenadiers had decided to fight to the death. For part of the time two Tigers from No. 2 Company of the 102nd Battalion supported their battle but by the morning of Thursday 17th a Canadian brigade had taken the railway station and were pushing towards the lateral road which runs on a general south-easterly line to Trun. The Tigers withdrew leaving behind in the school building controlling the Rue St Jean the survivors of the grenadiers who were to hold out until Friday and of whom only six survived the battle. Their stubborn defence had halted the drive of the 6th Canadian Brigade armour towards Necy.

While the isolated ss group was holding at bay the Canadian infantry and tanks the remnants of the main battle groups were withdrawn during the night of the 16th/17th to a new line which ran from Falaise to Morteaux–Coliboeuf pivoting on its left flank and eventually holding a line along a ridge. The selection of the position showed great appreciation of ground and weak though its units were the Hitler Youth was still preventing an Allied break-through eastwards or southwards. Just to the east of Falaise was the small village of Villy, set on the southern slope of a ridge above a river valley and surrounded by orchards. Tactically, it was important for it controlled a triangle of roads and Canadian attacks came in against it. Into this area, to support the small group of ss infantry which formed its garrison, rolled the combined remnants of 1st and 2nd Companies of the 102nd Tiger Battalion and took post on the northern edge of the village together with a pair of self-propelled guns which had also been sent post haste to bolster the defence.

During the early part of the afternoon a group of thirty or more 4th Canadian tanks made a reconnaissance in force against the village from Damblainville and through the shallow valley towards Villy. With the advantages of the upper ground and better observation to balance the odds against them the Tigers opened fire at long range, deflecting the attack and forcing the Canadians to the east where they forced a breach in the Hitler Youth line and drove rapidly southwards heading for Merri, at whose outskirts they were brought to a halt by a 9th ss battle group.

The whole front of the ss Division was a salient on either side of which the Canadian advance flowed steadily forward. One strong tank column had thrust down the Falaise road, now unprotected by any panzer or infantry, and was threatening Nécy; Merri was threatened and tanks of the Polish and Canadian forces were within 1½ km of Trun. The situation was rapidly deteriorating but there were still unexpected successes to be gained and one of these befell the defenders of Villy. In the early evening the ss were surprised to see a Canadian convoy of petrol lorries, escorted by a vedette of tanks approaching their position apparently unaware that although the advance had pushed on southwards on either side of the village, Villy itself was still in German hands. An armoured car and three petrol bowsers were destroyed and the escorting tanks forced to withdraw.

Far to the east the neck of the pocket was being slowly narrowed as the Poles strove to bring the advance forward to Chambois and thereby to bottle in the trapped German forces. Unexpectedly the Luftwaffe made its appearance on the battle-field during the early morning of the 17th, machine gunning the Polish vehicles and by desperate assault hoping to slow the advance. Late that evening they flew again over Jort this time bombing and hit some of the command vehicles of the Polish 10th Brigade. The advance was only slightly delayed and once the German machines had flown away was immediately resumed.

All the efforts of the Allies were now directed upon the capture of Trun. The Polish 10th Mounted Rifles breasted one hill from whose crown they should see far to the south flashes of artillery fire as American and French artillery batteries fired upon the town and upon the convoys of German lorries streaming through the narrow streets. Trun was a principal route of escape with one major and two minor roads heading out of the pocket, and all the roads were choked with traffic which was under almost continual bombardment by artillery and attacks by aircraft. But if the Germans were hard pressed they were still capable of offering the most determined resistance and late in the afternoon the Poles of No. 1 Squadron of 10th Mounted Rifles in their cross country advance from Les Moutiers-en-Auge ran into a battery of 8.8 cm guns which soon smashed back the Polish advance. Four Cromwells were hit and began to burn within seconds of reaching the crest of one hill and soon only two tanks were left in the squadron.

During the evening of Thursday the new c.-in-c. West, Field Marshal Model, the 'Saviour of the Eastern Front', arrived to take over from Kluge. He had come to exhibit on the Western Front the same skill in forming a firm and cohesive battle line from a disastrous break-through which he had shown in Russia. Like all new brooms he was determined to sweep clean but the situation he found defeated even him.

The pocket containing the German forces was rapidly diminishing in area. From the west the combined strengths of an American and British Armies which had linked at Briouze were pushing the German remnants eastwards. On the southern front, as we have seen, a firm and solid anvil of American and French forces had hemmed these remnants in and on the eastern front the jaws of the Allied pincers had nearly closed at Chambois and Trun. The northern wing had numerous salients where one formation stronger than the rest was holding a line deep in the British flank, or where some unit, overrun by numerical superiority, had given way and allowed the Allied armour to sweep forward. The main effort of the Allies was directed towards the shoulders of the neck of the pocket – the town of Trun and the village of Chambois – and it was obvious therefore that these would have to be held.

The only remaining question was to find forces to hold these vital areas. Although the maps at Supreme Command Headquarters West showed flags which represented divisions, corps and armies within the pocket there was no longer any proper command structure, no system of reliefs or supplies, none of the organization upon which the military depends and yet it was out of this chaos that order would have be restored just as it was from the troops within the pocket that the soldiers and weapons would have to come to restore it.

For days past the country roads, paths and tracks leading eastwards across

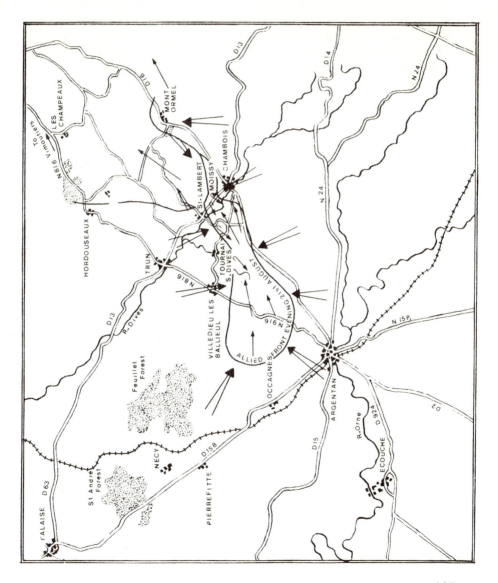

the Dives river had been choked with convoys escaping from the pocket but these were, for the greatest part, unorganized detachments. Now the High Command ordered that whole formations would be drawn *en bloc* and with minimum delay out of the front line, taken east of the Dives, reformed, refreshed and sent back in again to hold open the corridor through which the trapped units might escape.

The 2nd ss Panzer Corps was chosen for the task of breaking out eastwards and then to attack westwards back into the pocket, and the orders for its withdrawal out of the pocket had been issued on 16 August. On the afternoon of the 17th the main force passed through the burning streets of Trun.

With the decision to remove that corps the fighting now passed from the holding stage and entered upon its last phase, and was concentrated around a road only 7 km long and across which were only a handful of minor lateral roads. This was the vital area in which the most bitter fighting was to take place, for although there were still battles being fought along the length and breadth of the pocket it had become clear that the fate of the armies depended upon the 7 km stretch of road from Trun to Chambois being kept open.

Thus with the dawn of Friday 18 August we close this account of the fighting on the northern flank. During that day the 12th ss was to fight to retain its hold on Nécy, a straggling village in the valley of a small river but one which controlled a network of minor roads along which the armies could retreat. The remnants of 102nd Tiger Battalion were preparing to move forward from l'Abbaye to Nécy to support the Hitler Youth, the 85th Division had been forced north and eastwards and was, therefore, now outside the pocket. The 89th Division was a battered rump and to all intents and purposes, militarily useless.

For the fifteen German divisions streaming towards the few exits from the pocket there was to be, during the early morning of Friday 18 August, a brief respite from the aircraft which had followed them on their long, slow haul from Mortain. The day had dawned cold and misty, a day of low cloud which not only inhibited flying but hiding from the view of the Allied artillery the roads and paths along which the congested columns were moving out of a pocket which had been by late evening reduced to a length of only 10 km and a width of 12.

At High Command level von Kluge had left for Germany and Model was to begin a conference during that morning with his senior field commanders at the chateau of Fontaine l'Abbé, but his ideas could only be a restatement of von Kluge's – a withdrawal from the pocket through a neck held at the south by Chambois and in the north at Trun. Then came the news that 2nd Canadian Division had captured Trun. Now the corridor was only 7 km wide and the crossing points across the Dives could be counted on the fingers of one hand.

The Eastern Flank

'The 2nd SS Panzer Corps ... will attack and will break open the ring between Trun and Chambois'.
Orders to 2nd and 9th ss Divisions, 19 August 1944

All through the night of 17/18 August the tanks and lorried infantry of 1st Polish Armoured Division had been driving. Late in the evening had come the order for them to close the gap around the German armies, and if they were to accomplish this then Chambois must be attacked and taken and a link-up made with the Americans or French who were fighting south of the village.

The selection of the Poles as the army to close the ring around this, the first major encirclement of German troops in Normandy, was perhaps deliberate for this was the month in which five years before the war had begun and this operation was the first real opportunity for the Poles to repay in kind the destruction which had been wrought against them. To the Poles this order to lead the 2nd Canadian Corps in a race to close the gap had come as a signal honour and so great was the eagerness of the tired soldiers and officers to begin the attack that many of the tanks set off without having refuelled or re-ammunitioned. The 2nd Armoured Regiment with the 8th Infantry Battalion formed the point unit and without waiting for a guide they drove off into the starlit night.

The terrain through which they passed was more steep than that over which they had been fighting for the past weeks. The narrow country tracks meandered, following the easiest lines of ascent up the hills. There could be no deviation from many of these tracks as they passed through cuttings enclosed by high wooded banks. In the dark each wooded hill looked the same and so slowly the column began to move north-eastwards into the high country around Coudehard and not south-westwards towards Chambois.

It was this mistake in navigation that led the Poles to debouch out of a side road and nearly to collide with a column moving slowly forward on a south/north drive. The Poles were surprised at seeing so many vehicles for they thought that they were the only night travellers. The Polish commander ordered that headlights be switched on and in the light it was seen that the column was a German one heading towards Mount Ormel. The Poles reacted immediately and opened fire, while the Germans, who had not been expecting an interception so deep into what they thought was their territory, at first scattered but then regrouped and began to reply to the Polish bombardment.

It was, however, a one-sided fight for the panzer could not deploy and the Poles both could and did. Within half an hour the road was littered with broken and burning vehicles, dead men and horses. The Poles swung on to the south-north road the better to pursue and overtake other German columns. The surprise was successful in every case and the few challenges which did ring out during that wild night drive were answered with gun-fire. But this drive was taking the exultant Poles even farther away from their objective and dawn on 18 August found the leaders of the point unit at Champeaux on the 250 m line and far from Chambois. At Champeaux there were targets enough. In the small houses of the village the headquarters of 2nd ss Panzer Division had been set up and the entrance to the village blocked by a barricade defended by bazooka grenadiers and backed by an 8.8 cm gun. The road block was rushed and destroyed and the 88 smashed before it had fired a shot. The Shermans and Cromwells rolled across the ruins of the road block and down the village street. They turned right and there on the road before them was a marching company of grenadiers heading out of the encirclement. Within seconds not a single German soldier was left alive.

The Polish column had become dangerously lengthened and was soon under fire from the 'Das Reich' grenadiers and panzers of that division. Under this fierce bombardment the armoured spearhead withdrew down the steep slopes at the eastern end of the village, into the valley of a small river, and by traversing the flank of the high ground arrived at Coudehard and halted there to regroup and take stock of their situation. At Coudehard they were within striking distance of Chambois, and the bombardments and attacks which they were suffering indicated that their location was an obstacle to the withdrawal of the 7th Army and that it was certain that the most determined efforts would be made by the Germans to clear them from the road. Under increasing pressure the Poles withdrew on to the high ground to the north west of Mount Ormel and into a small copse in which they rested and waited for fresh orders.

That the spirit of the Poles had been raised by the victories which they were achieving after so many weeks of combat can be imagined and an example of this can be seen in the attack by detachments of Dragoons and 24th Lancers which in a reconnaissance sweep in the pre-dawn, east of Louvières-en-Auge, identified and charged into the attack against four self-propelled guns. The light Polish vehicles of the Dragoon Troop thrust through the apple orchards heading towards the German gun line and although shells from the sps destroyed two of the charging vehicles the pace of the advance brought the Poles to within point blank range and they destroyed one of the sps. As the others withdrew they were taken in enfilade by the Shermans of the Lancers in hull-down position and were destroyed one after the other. These had been the last four sp guns of the artillery component of 1st ss Panzer Division 'Leibstandarte ss Adolf Hitler'; now that division's artillery had been reduced to light field pieces.

Polish patrols ranged wide across the countryside firing at groups of German soldiers and often themselves coming under infantry and artillery fire. Mortar bombs, armour-piercing shells, rocket propelled mortars and panzerfaust were the accompaniment to every attack which the Poles made or which were made upon them and despite their terrible tiredness and the strain of battle there was no time for sleep; the area to be covered was so large, the German units moving through it so numerous and the Poles so few in number that every man was put into the reconnaissance and sweeps which were essential.

For the Germans the 18th of August brought a serious deterioration in their situation. The hitherto orderly withdrawal of the units which had been holding the walls was caught up in a maelstrom of the mixed groups from every flank, all trying to use one of the few escape routes. With the pocket so small in extent (it now measured only 10 km long by 12 wide) there could no longer be a northern, western, southern or eastern flank. Now there was only the eastern with, as its shoulders, the town of Trun and the village of Chambois.

The intentions of the Canadian Corps Commander had changed from a mere cutting of the Trun–Chambois road and he had flung out formations to the east of this to cut the minor road which runs from Trun to Vimoutiers intending thereby to block the route of the German armies trying to drive up it.

The 4th Canadian Division swung out on a wide flank and passed through an area held only by shattered units which had escaped from the encirclement and thought themselves safe. The arrival of the Canadians confounded them and dispersed them so that only minimal resistance was encountered. The Poles not only had a wider flanking operation to undertake but also that of closing the gap between themselves in the north and the Americans in the south.

But we have seen how, by error, the Poles having advanced farther to the east than had been ordered were already carrying out, unwittingly, the first part of the Corps Commander's intention. The order to link up with the Americans would mean for them a cross-country move through almost mountainous terrain and across the front of the withdrawing but still potent Germans.

The fighting which then took place east of the Trun–Chambois road was concentrated chiefly around that piece of high ground which has passed into Polish military history. This ground is between Mount Ormel and Coudehard and connects one Point 262 to the other Point 262 south of the Mount and nearer to Chambois. The shape of the contour lines has the appearance of a mace with the handle in the south and the head in the north, and this odd configuration gave to that feature the name by which it is known to Polish historians.

The ground around Chambois rises sharply from the 100 m line and carries a secondary road from that village eastwards through Mount Ormel and then on towards Vimoutiers and the Seine river. Mount Ormel and the two Points 262 lay across the German escape route and afforded excellent observation westwards towards the valley of the Dives and northwards towards the Champeaux hills east of Trun. Possession of this high ground was essential and it can be readily understood why in the fighting in the last days of the pocket the mace assumed a sinister significance and the fighting a bitterness which had not been encountered throughout the whole time of the encirclement.

It was the 18th day of August and the struggle was to last three more days. By 21 August the main break-out had been made and only stragglers were to be met moving through the woods and orchards, avoiding the Allied patrols and heading always eastwards, hoping to reach the German lines. The 7th Army and the 5th Panzer Army were at the end of their military careers in Normandy, but for the next seventy-two hours they were to be involved in fighting of the most desperate savagery, incredible losses and sacrifices on an heroic scale.

The reasons for such desperation lie in the fact that there was now only a handful of escape routes and while the Polish divisional commander issued his orders to move on Chambois and to capture the Mace, thereby cutting one road, his colleague commanding the Canadian Division gave orders that St Lambert-sur-Dives, a small village, approximately midway between Trun and Chambois, was to be captured by a task force thus cutting the last escape route. The execution of these orders would place small Allied groups athwart the line of the German withdrawal and those Allied detachments would be subject to the most severe attacks by men determined at all costs to escape death or captivity.

But before we concentrate upon the fighting east of the Trun–Chambois road let us review the situation in the pocket within whose confines there was complete and utter confusion. In fact, it would be true to say that the period from 18 to 21 August 1944, was, to many who lived through it, more terrible for the constricted space in which the units were held between the de Gouffern Woods and the swampy bed of the Dives river than for the fighting which took place. It will be remembered that the ordered withdrawal from the western side of the pocket had resulted in severe congestion of the roads leading down to the steep banked valley of the Orne river across which there was only a single bridge. The British had attacked Montpinçon and had gone on to capture Rouvres, Soumont and Tournebû against desperate resistance. The us forces had advanced past Briouze and as a result of the capture of Argentan the distance between the Allied pincer points was only 18 km. The night of 17/18 August had seen the orderly withdrawal of much of the German Train along the Putanges–Pierrefitte road and into the area of Nécy where it was concentrating before making a final move towards the escape routes. In and around Nécy were concentrated the headquarters of two armies and four corps.

During the 18th there was fresh British pressure against Nécy and Hausser, General Officer Commanding 7th Army, was so often attacked by aircraft during one of his car journeys that he was forced to abandon the vehicle and to complete the trip on foot. He arrived at 84th Corps headquarters tired after a long and exhausting walk along ditches.

His orders were that 84th Corps was to be placed directly under army control and that it was to take command of all troops on the northern side of the pocket. This would simplify the command structure. Corps was then to guard Army by setting up defensive positions north of the Ronay–Corday line. The task of sealing off the British penetrations at Nécy was given to the weak elements of 84th Division which were slowly seeping into the area. Every sort of splinter unit which arrived into 84th Corps sector was brought into service and by using elements from 3rd Para. Division a thin but firm line of posts was established north of the line Brieux–Nécy.

Further to the south the II ss Panzer Corps together with 8th and 9th Mortar Brigade had been withdrawn from the line at Argentan and had been ordered to form Army reserve at Lisieux, but the deteriorating situation, particularly the danger that the Allies would cut the 5th Panzer and 7th Armies off forced a change of orders. It had been decided that strong forces from outside the pocket would attack at the Allies' weakest point and break open an escape corridor through which the bulk of the German forces could withdraw. The movement of the II Panzer Corps into reserve was cancelled and it was ordered instead to leave the encirclement by two roads and to regroup in the Vimoutiers area before striking south-westwards towards Trun, the place considered by German intelligence officers to be the weakest spot in the Allied ring. The wording of the order showed how little contact with the real situation there was at Supreme Command, for okw had now taken upon itself to determine the roads which units might use. It was obviously unaware that there were only two roads left from which a withdrawal might be made and both of these were choked with convoys of troops and vehicles. For all its interference okw omitted to tell II ss Panzer Corps that in order to reach the stated concentration area at Vimoutiers it would have to fight its way through a strong and well-armed enemy holding a superior tactical position.

The ss Corps Commander, more aware of the true situation on the ground, gave orders that his two marching columns would move by daylight thus accepting the risk that they might be attacked en route. Barely had the columns begun their move eastward than a report was received that the Canadians had broken through the Falaise front with a strong armoured force.

The right-hand column moving from Nécy via Merri to Trun passed along its route without being diverted but the left-hand group was attacked by Canadian Shermans striking out of Bierre, immediately southwest of Merri. Orders went out for the left-hand column of 9th ss Panzer Division to regroup and to attack the Canadians and to drive them back towards Morteaux.

This was an order easier to give than to fulfil for by the time that it had been issued both the divisional columns had already become deeply entangled with other groups moving down the road. There was no wireless communication with the ss units and the right-hand column, made up of most of the Corps armour, was unaware of the 7th Army Commander's order. The dispersals brought about by the continual Allied air assaults, the inability of units and sub-units to communicate with each other and the general confusion which obtained meant that the right-hand column could not be brought into the attack at Morteaux and thus the fighting was left entirely to the left-hand group.

In order to bring their units out of the chaos of the withdrawal and to put them into the assault ss officers of the left-hand group took control of the situation on the roads ordering the slower moving vehicles, the horse-drawn guns and all the paraphernalia of the Train to drive into the fields or on to the side of the road so that the ss armour could get through. It was a situation which did not always meet with understanding. 'We thought that the ss were trying to save themselves at our expense. Their officers and NCOs carrying pistols and machine pistols moved up and down the convoy, all the time shouting orders: clear the way, move over there. We wondered why they weren't holding the battle line instead of bullying their way through.'

In an attempt to thicken the forces with which would attack the Canadian tank incursion the commander of a 'Hohenstaufen' panzergrenadier battalion intercepted and absorbed into his command any stragglers which passed through the area. To bolster the fragmenting front a handful of ss grenadiers and a pair of Tigers were sent to give aid. Some Luftwaffe flak guns and a few panzer, as well as splinter groups of infantry, were taken on charge and put into the line.

Within a short space of time these remnants had built a blocking line north west of Merri which held until the main divisional columns had reached Trun. Such was the overall deterioration that it was the strength of personality of individual men which held the dying front together: that and the personal initiative on the part of quite junior officers and of other ranks. There was no strategy in 7th Army's handling of the situation; just a patching of holes in the defence. Generals had long since ceased to control the movements of whole corps of divisions and were directing the tactical operations of battle groups often less than a battalion in strength. On either side of the pocket walls, along the battle line to the Dives river and beyond, the battle raged as the Allies, scenting victory and the chance to destroy the Germans in Normandy, concentrated their forces and redoubled their efforts.

East of Merri the 9th ss divisional columns had at last reached Trun and had begun the ascent of the high ground to reach Vimoutiers. The continual stopping en route, the clogged roads, the incessant air assaults had all played their part in separating the units of the Division from each other and it was only as individual and isolated groups that the detachments from 2nd ss Panzer and 9th ss Panzer Divisions finally arrived in their concentration area and prepared for their counter-attack back into the pocket.

In order that not one machine which might possibly be used was left in Allied hands the workshop company of 102nd Panzer Battalion towed lightly damaged vehicles, sometimes in tandem, up the steep road to Vimoutiers. At Trun there was chaos and, once again, the ss officers had moved other traffic into side roads and on to the pavements of the narrow streets to allow the ss panzers and guns through. When the II ss Corps went through on 17 August Trun had not yet fallen to the Canadians and detachments from both the 9th ss and the 116th Panzer Divisions were still fighting to hold the Allied Shermans at the edge of the town. Shell-fire had set fire to a number of houses; others had been set alight by petrol bowsers, ammunition lorries and the spread of the conflagration from one house to another. The air above the town was choked with smoke which burned the eyes of the drivers peering through windscreens as they followed the tailboard of the vehicle in front but concealed from the Allied pilots the confusion which reigned below.

The small, narrow roads of Trun met at the Grand Place in the centre of the town and into this square, from all the traffic-choked side roads, oozed slowly carts, armoured personnel carriers, tanks, soft-skinned lorries, staff cars and foot columns. Thanks to the determined efforts of their junior officers the ss vehicles were swung left out of the town and reached the Vimoutiers road. There the congestion was if anything worse, for this was one of only four crossing points which the train and fighting troops of fifteen German divisions could still use. And all the time the Spitfires of the RAF rose and swooped over the columns, cannon guns supplemented the work of destruction which the Typhoons had carried out with rockets and bombs. Slowly, inch by inch, the German columns four-deep intermingled with groups of men, guns, horses and vehicles strove to achieve the Mount Ormel heights pursued by the RAF, harried by the artillery, unaware that very soon their columns were to be under attack from the Poles.

Despite the chaos which obtained it must not be considered that the Germans were either powerless to defend themselves, too bemused to plan ahead or too weak to carry out the requirements of a military existence. Each attack which they launched was properly mounted; each patrol was briefed and every reconnaissance had a purpose. Even if command from the centre was nearly always inoperable due to the lack of communications and to the swiftly changing pattern of events, the lower echelons kept the military machine rolling by carrying out the routine tasks.

One such military duty was the policing of the Trun–Vimoutiers road for which the 9th ss Pioneer Battalion and elements of the divisional panzer battalion had been selected. Their task was not only to keep the road open so that traffic flowed freely but also to fight back the attempts of the Allies to cut it. The pioneers and their vehicles cruised up the ruler-straight road observing the results of the Allied air strikes and removing from the road the debris – vehicular and human – which would have obstructed the free flow.

As the pair of Panzer IV and a self-propelled gun, which formed the unit's spearhead, emerged from Hordouseaux village they came under fire from a vedette of Polish Cromwells moving forward on their own reconnaissance. Without halting the panzer moved forward with guns firing but then the ss troop noticed that behind the Polish point were drawn up the squadrons of an entire regiment ready to advance. The three German armoured vehicles entered into battle and for two hours the unequal struggle lasted but the Polish point unit eventually withdrew upon its parent body and the road was re-opened. During the night of 17th/18th the Pioneer Battalion reached Vimoutiers to join up with other detachments which had been seeping in throughout the day. By halfway through the 18th the bulk of 9th ss had reached the concentration area. Behind them the road had been cut again, part of the division was still fighting in vain to prevent the fall of Trun and with the loss of that place only the crossings at St Lambert, Moissy and Chambois still led the way out of the trap.

Against the mass of material and men which the British, Poles, Canadians, Americans and French were throwing into the attack the Germans had only the courage of desperation. The 12th ss fought fanatically for every feature; each eminence became a strong point for whose possession short fire fights and bitter hand to hand fighting took place.

Against the flank at Nécy the British put in 53rd (Welsh) Division, a new formation on that sector and one eager to come to grips with the Germans. The Welsh *élan* brought them storming forward but against the ss and the tactics which they had evolved the bravery of the Welsh was of no avail and their first assaults were flung back with heavy loss.

Part of the 102nd Panzer Battalion which had been withdrawn during the night of 17th/18th to a point a few kilometres south of Fresnay was ordered to link up with a handful of self-propelled guns, which took up position on the right flank, and to move against strong British forces which were striking down to La Hoguette. Part of the panzer battalion moved to a point west of l'Abbaye and in an effort to increase the fire power of the little group one

Tiger towed another whose engine had broken down. With the immobile vehicle in position at the southern edge of l'Abbaye a second Tiger was driven to the north-west exit of the village and a pair of sp guns came up to add muscle to the defence.

Late in the afternoon the British sent in a tank attack across the gently sloping uplands, its approach from Pertheville-Ners hidden for some time by a crescent-shaped copse of trees. Then the British armoured fighting vehicles came into sight and into range. The fighting was short and intense; the Tiger on the north-western edge of the village supported by the sp guns broke up the assault.

While this little engagement was being fought No. 1 Tiger Company of 102nd Battalion had been battling against Allied tank assaults on the Falaise–Argentan road, and the remaining panzers of 10th ss Division were drawn into the battle. At last light the Tigers around l'Abbaye and around Nécy were ordered to withdraw and the immobile Tiger on the southern edge of l'Abbaye was blown up.

As the two Tigers of 102nd Panzer Battalion which had formed the backbone of the defence moved out they were joined by a third and together they started back to Nécy. *En route* one was struck by an anti-tank gun shell and burst into flames; the second collided with the third and both vehicles were so badly damaged that they had to be abandoned. Thus, unspectacularly and clumsily, died the 102nd Independent Tiger Tank Battalion.

To support the isolated group of ss grenadiers on the Nécy sector there now remained only the weak divisional artillery for which little ammunition was coming forward. Slowly the gun-fire died away and emboldened by the silence of the German artillery the British infantry stormed forward again and drove the ss out of their positions. Slowly groups of grenadiers withdrew across country, turning at bay whenever the pursuing British infantry came too close, always losing men through casualties, but conducting the best type of fighting withdrawal. Some groups, less fortunate than others, were cut off by Cromwells and Stuarts and died under the tank tracks fighting the armour with close combat weapons.

Behind the grenadier line lay divisional headquarters, the only command group of 12th ss Division still active. The men of the intermediate command headquarters, regimental and battalion, had long since been absorbed into the firing line. Nor was there any longer a divisional administrative 'tail'. Every man who could fire a gun or use a panzerfaust was in the line. The train and the divisional heavy weapons group had arrived somewhere near the neck of the pocket and were to be embroiled in the confused fighting of the last days, trying hard to hold open the route of escape so that other formations might escape. Far to the west there was still a small outpost of the ss fighting in the Falaise Ecole Supérieure. Although their numbers were few two of them had been sent by the remainder to break through to Division and to bring the last messages. In the afternoon of the 18th the four surviving grenadiers from the group of sixty which had formed the garrison of the école, came out of the rubble and surrendered.

The 19th of August dawned bright and sunny, forecasting a day of aerial attacks, in contrast to that of the 18th when low cloud and mist had hampered the Allied air assault. It was only in the afternoon of the 18th that the air forces had been able to attack the 7th Army, but in the few remaining hours of light had flown 1,471 missions against the shrinking pocket, an indication of the importance which the Falaise area had gained. The whole sector was choked with columns whose progress was impeded by military wreckage, the result of previous raids. The aircraft swooping above the convoys did not need to select a target, everything below them was fair game. The 84th Corps in its reports for the 19th remarked that in its opinion the air assaults had been less frequent and intense and advanced the theory that this reduction had been caused not only by the dust cloud which hung motionless in the air, hiding from the Allied pilots the columns which were their targets, but also because the Allied air forces were already attacking targets along the Seine and could leave the destruction of the troops in the pocket to the fury of the guns.

The 84th Corps that morning was without troops, orders or intelligence appreciations, although it was known that the Allies were on the Dives river and, therefore, were in the Army's rear. Later in the forenoon unconfirmed and inaccurate news was received that relief attempts by troops outside the pocket to smash the ring open and thereby release the encircled armies had failed. In view of this each unit was ordered to act independently and with dispatch to regain the German lines, and carrying out the heaviest weapons possible, for strong forces would be needed to hold back the 3rd US Army whose advance towards the line of the Eure river was threatening the formation of a second, and larger, pocket around Rouen.

The Corps' supply lorries began to move out at 12.30 hrs leaving behind only those sections of the headquarters which had been ordered to remain with 7th Army. The first destination was Bailleul but even before the motorized convoys had reached any distance from the start line area they had been caught up in the slow-paced convoys and were hemmed in from all sides.

Air defence against the Allied aircraft was conducted by the drivers and escort personnel who rushed into the fields of harvested corn and opened fire behind the corn stooks with rifles and machine guns upon the low flying aircraft. When the road passed through the great wooded areas where the vehicles were hidden from sight there was indescribable confusion as each driver tried to increase speed and to overtake the vehicle in front. There were lorry columns cutting across the main body, others which tried to force themselves into the main group, and others which set out to cross the ground between the trees. The whole area of the road through the woods soon turned into a morass and those vehicles which tried to avoid the mud by diverting across country frequently came to grief when tree stumps smashed their oil casings and sumps. Once again officers had to resort to threats with pistols to force the less important traffic off the road so that the guns and armour could pass through. Despite the conditions within the pocket and the certain knowledge that this was the last chance to escape certain death or captivity there was no panic, although there was a certain loosening of the strictest forms of discipline.

Once it was out of the woods the column descending the narrow country road towards the Dives river was in full view of the Allied artillery observers. As the vehicles moved slowly on they knew that every turn of the wheel would bring them under fiercer and more accurate artillery fire. They were, in effect, charging the guns – but in slow, very slow motion. The columns passed through the burning Bailleul and then crossed the Dives at St Lambert, and once word had been sent back that the trucks of 84th Corps had escaped then the Quartermaster's Department and the other sections of the HQ were ordered to follow. Corps then received the message informing it that its immediate tasks had been accomplished and that it had been dissolved as a formation HQ. A new concentration area was given it north of Mount Ormel in which it would take up fresh duties forming a cachement line near Amiens.

The Corps Commander attended his last conference and found from the situation map that the whole German force was concentrated into a rough square which ran from Trun via Brieux to Ronay and from Neuvy to Tableauville. This was 74th Corps sector and from Pierrefitte to Occagnes was held by II Para. Corps. The area north of Argentan to Chambois and thence to the heights south of Trun was controlled by 47th Panzer Corps. The greatest Allied pressure was being made against the battle group of 363rd Division which had the task of maintaining the front across the Falaise–Argentan road and of keeping the flanks against the British striking down from the north and against the Americans driving up from the south. Behind this shield the other units were carrying out their slow-paced withdrawal.

During the morning Simonds, the Canadian Corps Commander, ordered that the encirclement must be made complete and that no Germans were to escape. The Poles were ordered to strike for Chambois where they would link up with the Americans. The Canadians were to stop the neck of the last remaining major route by occupying the village of St Lambert-sur-Dives. From the German side there are virtually no accounts of the fierce fighting which took place in and around that place from Saturday 19 to Tuesday 22 August, but some indication of the value placed upon the action by the 21st

Army can be seen in the fact that Major Currie, the commander of the small combat group of tanks and infantry which advanced up and held St Lambert, was awarded the Victoria Cross.

Major Currie's group drove into the village after fighting its way through a strong German defence backed by 88s and halted. And at first light on Saturday the 19th he renewed the attack against the German garrison which had been reinforced during the night by a Tiger and a Panzer IV. Bitter fighting lasted throughout the day and then at last light the Canadian group was concentrated into a small group of houses. During Sunday Major Currie's last remaining officers were killed, but the fighting was at first no longer quite as fierce as it had been.

Late in the afternoon there were, however, signs that the Germans intended to make a counter-attack, backed this with a Panzer IV and covered it by a barrage from an 8.8 cm gun. The Canadian Shermans opened fire on the 88 and then fired into houses in which the German assault infantry had been grouped. The German attack was aborted. On Monday 21 August a change in the tempo of the fighting indicated that the German attacks were dying down and by Tuesday, with his task completed, Major Currie returned to his regiment, wondering, as he passed through the clutter of equipment, dead horses, wounded, dying and dead Germans, how it was possible that such devastation could have been wrought in so short a space of time.

But while Major Currie was still fighting his way forward to place himself squarely across the escape route at St Lambert the Poles had linked up with the Americans and a patrol from 10th Mounted Rifle Regiment entered Chambois at 19.00 hrs, to meet a rifle company of 359th Regiment from 90th Division. The ring was closed, however tenuously, and almost as a signal an Allied barrage of unprecedented fury fell upon all the road junctions in the Ballieul sector and sealed these off. There was now no longer any need for air assaults; the Allied guns could finish the task. From that time on each individual vehicle on the Trun–Villedieu–Argentan road was under fire. Even small groups of soldiers, and sometimes individual men, were bombarded. Any movement in the German lines drew artillery fire from the north, east and south. Darkness was the only friend of the escaping columns, darkness and the muscle power of the draught horse. Horse-drawn carts and guns were taken off the road and across country, traversing in the dark the bare ground in front of Tournai.

Army issued orders during the evening of the 19th that the break-out from the encirclement would be made during the coming night. In view of the difficulties of relaying detailed instructions – the telephone wires had been cut to pieces and the temperamental wireless sets would not work – each unit was to act independently, but control over the escape on the northern sector would be conducted by the staff of 84th Corps.

The commanders of both 84th and II Para. Corps expressed doubts about the break-out plan, which laid down that their forces were to escape via Trun, for they both considered that the strongest enemy resistance would be met at that point. Army then changed the point of the escape thrust and allowed II Para. to break out on either side of St Lambert. They ordered 84th Corps as well as 74th Corps, whose men were holding the western wall, to follow II Para. through the gap.

We leave then the huddled groups of German soldiers along the Trun–Chambois road, rocked by shell blast and bombarded almost at leisure by the Allied artillery, and return to the 12th ss who during 19 August were to play a significant part in holding back the Allied drive to break down the shoulders of the pocket.

A dawn attack by British infantry began 19 August for the remnants of 12th ss and this strong assault on the left of the grenadiers broke through their line. Into the gap which had been created poured a flood of British armour. Soon the divisional headquarters at Nécy had come under direct attack and was overrun. The ss survivors joined Krause battle group in new positions south east of the railway line. To relieve the pressure upon the grenadiers Max Wünsche led the last panzer detachment out into the attack. The odds against them were enormous and the Allied armoured power too great for them to overcome.

They had carried out battles against overwhelming odds so many times that this situation was normal to them and their tactics were those we had used on the Eastern Front. The panzer would be revved up and would roar forward with all guns blazing. We knew that the Allies felt a sense of inferiority when faced by Tigers and we depended a lot on this moral effect. Wünsche's group roared away and soon were lost in clouds of dust and smoke. They charged into the enemy who had broken through and not one panzer returned. Wünsche, who had been awarded the Oak Leaves only a week before, was badly wounded and captured.

The gallant charge lasted only half an hour and was beaten into the ground. No crew escaped death, injury or captivity. The fighting was now being concentrated around single groups of men and Allied barrages were being directed against the grenadier positions.

North of Bierre and Roch the divisional headquarters' Defence Company and Olboeter battle group formed a line. We sent them a Flakpanzer with four 2 cm guns and two 15 cm assault guns. Then, a little later, two Panthers and six Flakpanzer. We were lucky that no massive enemy infantry attacks were launched. We could not have withstood them.

During the evening of the 19th, Division received information that a break-out was planned and that from Vimoutiers the II ss Panzer Corps was to begin a relief operation. The task of the Hitler Youth Division was to hold open the northern shoulder of the pocket and, subsequently, orders were received that when the break-out came the remnants of the HJ Division were to follow 3rd Para. There was little time left.

With the rapid constriction of the neck of the pocket each road, path and track had assumed a life and death importance. The minor road to Vimoutiers through the Mace had assumed such an importance for the side which held it and the Mace controlled the movement from Chambois eastwards. To the soldiers of 1st Polish Armoured Division was given, as we have seen, the task of seizing and holding the Mace and of linking up with the Americans in the south.

The strain of fighting had told upon the Poles for they had been in action, almost without rest, throughout the long hot August days and had hoped that perhaps they might be given a day or so of peace in which they could rest themselves and give their tanks the maintenance which they so badly needed. Their new orders were to set them off into a fierce and brutal battle: into combat experiences so dramatic that a memorial to the fallen was designed and erected to commemorate the bitterness of the battle. But for 18 August the main portion of the Division was still girding itself to renew the struggle and only a small tank and armoured car reconnaissance group was active on the Polish divisional southern flank, moving into position to protect the wings of those units which were to assault the Mace on the morrow.

In a field near Jort No. 3 Battery of the ss Flak Battalion had received orders to move out and to regroup nearer to divisional headquarters. Some of the guns had been limbered up ready to move when the Cromwells of a Polish squadron poured over the crest of the hill and swept down upon them. The surprise was mutual and the reaction immediate. The Poles, true to their cavalry tradition, charged the guns, firing their own tank cannon as they roared, careering from side to side, down the shell-cratered slopes. The crews of a pair of 88s which were still ready for action rushed to man the guns and within seconds had swung the barrels round to face the advancing tanks. While the remainder of the battery pulled away and withdrew through a tree line and out of sight the two flak guns and a handful of grenadiers armed with panzerfaust and machine guns gave them covering fire. The 88s sent salvo after salvo crashing towards the Polish armour and with their final shots destroyed a Sherman but then the tanks were in among the ss, shooting down the gunners and grenadiers, overrunning the weapon pits and destroying the guns. The Polish advance flowed on across the now-silent artillery positions, striking along the boundary between the 12th ss and 85th Division. Ahead of the Polish armour there was no cohesive defence, nothing which could have halted a determined unit from advancing to draw tight the noose around the neck of the pocket. Surprisingly the Polish

Reconnaissance Troop halted and consolidated its positions, but then slowly resumed the advance and drove down the right flank of the ss Division heading southwards and eastwards.

Along the sectors of the 12th ss front other divisional components were being destroyed piecemeal. The Hauk reconnaissance group went down in a flurry of tank shells and machine gun fire and now each surviving grenadier fought on knowing that death was an almost certain and imminent fate. Along the Falaise–Argentan road the Canadians had struck down the ss Division's left flank and this penetration, coupled with that which the Poles had made down the right wing, had created an ss salient thrusting into the Allied line, a salient which was under attack along its entire length.

By 10.00 hrs on 19th the Poles had begun to move out in compliance with the Corps Commander's orders and swung out of the side road east of Ecorches undetected by the watchful German artillery observers, for a small stretch of woodland which covered both sides of the Trun–Vimoutiers road concealed the approach of the tanks as they moved towards Point 239. To the south west lay the whale-shaped, bare rise of the Mace and the 1st Polish Armoured regiment began its attack upon the northern side, or the 'head' of the feature.

The Rifle Companies of the Polish Highland Battalion went in to make a conventional infantry attack, moving with ease through the birch trees which dotted the hillside, and the pace of their advance passed over the German forward defence line. Then the armoured squadrons moved off, driving up the steep incline in low gear, the engines roaring with the strain of the slope. Individual troops of tanks moved along the sides of the feature to rest their overheating engines; others halted to give flank protection while the remainder struck forward to cut the Chambois–Vimoutiers road. The whole armoured regiment moved forward and then as it breasted a small rise halted in sheer astonishment. The road before it was a mass of slowly moving columns containing almost every type of vehicle, cart and armoured fighting machine serving with the German Army. Nose to tail the carts, lorries and panzers ground forward up the steep slope, struggling forward to reach the height and to descend into the safety that Vimoutiers meant to them.

To many of the Poles the revenge which they then exacted was payment for the great extermination battle in the bend of the Bzurza river where the mass of the Polish Army had been trapped and annihilated in just such a situation. The targets before them would now be destroyed as the Poles had been destroyed five years before. The 1st Polish Armoured Regiment deployed as if on parade, its move unheeded by the columns oozing past it. The first salvo fired at 12.45 hrs brought to the Germans the knowledge that the last major road of escape had been cut and for those between the Polish tank guns and Chambois there was no way out. Panzers trapped within the columns could not deploy and could only bring their guns to bear with the hope that within the limits of their traverse they could find and destroy an Allied target. Polish tanks ranged along the top of a small cutting in which a mixed horse and panzer column had been halted and systematically began to destroy it. The heat in the tanks was unbearable. The Polish Highland Infantry was fighting in a close and oppressive atmosphere made hotter, more oppressive and more unbearable by the heat from the burning vehicles and the choking clouds of smoke which slowly began to obscure the fearful sights of the destroyed column. A sudden torrential cloudburst obscured in driving flurries the more distant horrors and then as the rain stopped, as abruptly as it had begun, the tanks ceased fire and allowed those Germans who wished to surrender to be collected, those who were wounded to be dressed and those who despaired of fighting their way through the ring of steel to flood back again towards Chambois.

At Vimoutiers there had been a hubbub of activity since the order to II ss Panzer Corps had gone out and as the tired, hungry and fought-out men and vehicles had arrived guides had met them and led them into well-camouflaged bivouacs where they could rest, eat and sleep.

The workshop companies took over the vehicles, working throughout the nights under huge tarpaulins to hide them from the Allied aircraft, tuning up the engines, replacing parts and re-arming the vehicles.

All through the days which followed small groups of men and machines came in bearing the marks of the bitter fighting in which they had been engaged. A steady trickle of grenadiers and their panzer assembled to execute those orders which were issued during the evening of 19 August.

The II ss Panzer Corps will attack from the Vimoutiers sector in a westerly direction and will open the pocket between Trun and Chambois so as to allow the 7th Army to flow out eastwards. The following units will take part:

On the right: 9th ss Panzer Division in two combat groups will attack via St Gervais towards Louvières with one group, while the main group will strike via Champeaux to Trun.

On the left: The 2nd ss Panzer Division will attack St Lambert and Chambois via Champosoult.

The usual shortages of petrol delayed the preparations and the dramatic re-organization which was needed to form reasonably effective battle groups from the remnants which had arrived and were still arriving as late as last light on the 19th, led to a cancellation of the attack for that night. It was not until late in the night of 19th/20th that the assault groups moved forward into their concentration areas.

At dawn on the morning of 20 August, the ss counter-offensive opened.

This was a pale imitation of those tremendous advances in which the ss Divisions had taken part during their short lives but however weak may have been the units charging forward to open the Allied iron ring the feeling of battle, the joy of combat for the sake of combat animated many of the young soldiers and led to great acts of bravery and heroism throughout the counter-offensive.

The 9th ss Reconnaissance Battalion swung out along the narrow country road and through the copses, across the broken and difficult country via Crouttes to St Gervais des Sablons. The task of this understrength unit was to protect the northern flank of the main divisional thrust which would drive the Vimoutiers–Trun road and break the Polish blocks which had cut the highway. Between St Gervais and Champeaux the leading elements of 9th ss struck the rear echelons of the 2nd Polish Armoured Regiment as it was on its way to support the garrison on the Mace. The tanks and lorried infantry of 2nd Regiment together with a second infantry battalion as reinforcement were moving to take up position on the northern and eastern slopes of the Mace, and to thicken the Polish defence line against the attacks which were now coming in fast and furious. The bulk of the Polish Regiment took up its allotted area leaving behind a rear-guard which gave such a good account of itself that the forward advance of the 9th ss Division was temporarily halted. It soon became clear that the handful of panzer and sp guns under the ss command were insufficient to thrust aside the Polish armour; nor were the ss grenadiers numerous enough to engage the Polish lorried infantry with any success. The grenadiers had been among the last to arrive in the Vimoutiers concentration area and had had a scant six hours' sleep before moving out again in the counter-attack.

The northern ss pincer could not advance and the main thrust therefore passed to 2nd ss Division which was thrusting to reach Coudehard and Mount Ormel. Once again the weakness of the panzer units and the numerical inferiority of the grenadiers prevented the ss from achieving their objectives. To support 'Das Reich' the rocket propelled mortar battalion was formed into two battle groups and began a bombardment under which it was hoped the assaulting infantry would be able to rush the peaks.

The long, hot afternoon of 20 August saw one attack succeed another. Every combination of tactic was used: conventional infantry assault, combined panzer and grenadier, unsupported Panther attacks, savage bombardments or no barrage at all. Against each and every assault the Poles held firm. Some of the slopes of the Mace were so steep that the ss climbed them bent double and pulling at bushes to bring themselves forward; at other places the ground formed a natural hollow and into this killing ground poured the grenadiers driving for the summit and only to be shot down by machine guns on the tanks and blown apart by their shells. There comes a time in battle when the bitterness of the realization that bravery by itself cannot overcome armour or machine gun bullets drives the attacker to a black despair and forces him to charge forward once again in the hope that

145

this frenzy may yet succeed. In just such a lust did the ss grenadiers storm forward into one bitter assault during that terrible day. The few officers who had survived led them storming forward with the German battle cry 'UUUUURRRAAAA', forced out of their dry throats and heaving lungs as they stormed forward in a final endeavour. The Polish guns, hot from almost continual firing, opened up again and the last desperate charge was driven into the ground and died.

All that was left was to build up a strong line as far forward as possible to facilitate the flow of the escapers of 7th Army; there could now be no question of a break-through to the river Dives.

But the Poles did not only have to fight against the ss assaults coming in from the direction of Vimoutiers. The troops escaping from the encirclement were also making their own bid to force the Poles aside and in pursuit of this endeavour launched massive but un-coordinated attacks out of Chambois. German artillery fire opened a destructive and heavy fire during the afternoon of the 20th aiming to drive from off the open ground the Polish armour and infantry which held it and hoping to cover by the fury of the bombardment the stealthy attempts by other groups to escape through the Polish blocking line.

One of the first German attacks came in during the early morning of the 20th when two Panthers opened fire upon a Polish tank vedette, intending by this manoeuvre to cover the escape of parties of infantry. Within minutes two of the Polish machines had been hit and had begun to burn. On another sector an *ad hoc* battle group of German infantry was led into an attack by a Panzer IV and an armoured personnel carrier. At point blank range the carrier was hit and destroyed by a PIAT projector while a 17 pdr anti-tank gun engaged and destroyed the armoured fighting vehicle. Robbed of its armoured support the German infantry assault faltered and withdrew.

Through a countryside covered with German columns attempting to escape there were also small groups of Polish armour and vehicle convoys trying to reach, re-arm and resupply their units on Mount Ormel and clashes were frequent. There were losses on both sides and during one particularly vicious bombardment, during which some Polish three-tonners had been set alight, a platoon of Panzer Vs worked their way forward and upon emerging from a small wood opened fire upon the Polish Shermans. The range was just under a mile and with a speed born of despair the German tank gunners loaded and fired their 88s. In a matter of seconds five Shermans were alight and the remainder of the squadron withdrew to avoid further losses.

The whole air was alive with the noise of battle and the stench of it. Giant rocket propelled mortars whined and screeched and roared in a rising crescendo of screaming and all the time the unannounced medium mortar bombs fell, sometimes with precision and at other times at random over the length and breadth of the Polish positions. The Poles were caught between the attacking pincers of the Germans trying to escape from the pocket and those who were trying to break into it.

Behind every major and sustained barrage came the German infantry assaults, led with determination and executed with a lunatic fury in assaults which threatened more than once to sweep from the summit the Polish garrison whose numbers diminished with every fresh barrage and each new assault. Isolated and unsupported, for the Canadians were themselves embroiled in fighting of the most bitter type, the Poles stood and fought off each new attack. By now the Mace was surrounded and the Polish defenders had to stand and fight or die. There was no other alternative.

Near a Polish battalion headquarters a panzer and grenadier attack came in, the tank cannon and machine guns trying to blast a way through the Polish lines through which the German infantry could elude capture. The German machine gunners worked their way nearer to Polish headquarters opening fire with the fast-firing MG 42s not only at ground level but also from trees by snipers who had concealed themselves in the foliage. A Polish anti-tank gun, its crew lying dead round it, was brought into battle by some of the riflemen fighting nearby and with almost the first shot destroyed one of the Panzer IVs which were attacking the position. A second Polish gun fired from a flank and hit another tank which began to withdraw. A direct hit 'brewed up' the Panzer IV and the German grenadiers, baffled but not defeated, went to ground to wait for more armoured support to come up and force a passage through the Polish positions.

Panzer Vs came in against a second Polish battalion and under their assault the Polish line was dented and the battalion's carrier platoon lost. To support the German attack flocks of mortar bombs fell in, upon and around the Polish slit trenches. The SS infantry attacks were almost continuous. Assaults by individual panzer and by small groups then came in from every direction, sometimes alone but more usually accompanied by infantry who either went unescorted into battle or used the bulk of the armoured vehicles as shields from which to escape the encirclement.

Throughout the cool and overcast night of 20/21 August there was concern in the Polish battalions at the high level of ammunition which had been expended. None had been wasted, all targets had been legitimate but it was crystal clear that the Poles were isolated and standing like a rock in a tide of German activity.

There had been times during the afternoon of the 20th when the infantry assaults by grenadiers of the 'Das Reich' Division had nearly reached the summit of the Mace. One particularly vicious assault had been opened with a barrage of mortar bombs and rocket propelled 'Nebelwerfer' shells of enormous calibre. Under cover of this furious bombardment had come the Panthers clearing the way for the storm troops. These had charged uphill from their armoured personnel carriers, flinging grenades and firing their

147

assault machine pistols, covering the whole ground with fire. They had continued to advance, despite terrible losses, until it was clear that against the well dug-in Poles their *élan* would not succeed. The ss assault flowed down hill, was regrouped and brought forward, again and again, and each time with bitter loss. Suddenly it was all over and the German pressure was applied on other sectors, but not once did the pressure relent nor the assaults diminish in fury. General Meindl, the German Para. Corps Commander, was determined to wrest from the Polish grasp the vital heights around Mount Ormel.

The 21st brought no relief to the hard-pressed Poles. The view from their slit trenches must have depressed them terribly. Those on the left side of the hill could see passing below them, head to tail and terribly congested, the weary, green columns of the German Army while those on the right of the hill could see forming up for the attack fresh squadrons and companies of the ss, ready to begin yet another day of assault and counter-attack. One suicidal attack was launched against the right-hand defenders. An ss company of grenadiers stormed up the slippery, grassy slopes of the Mace shouting their battle cries and throwing their stick hand grenades. Into the sector under attack moved the tanks of the Polish anti-aircraft troop with their heavy machine guns. Within seconds the storm troops had fallen and the wounded were screaming as the grass ignited by the tanks' tracer bullets began to burn around them. This was almost the last infantry assault and as the German grenadier assaults ebbed away so did the artillery diminish in intensity and the everlasting mortars at last lessen their attentions. The Poles had held the Mace against the blows from the II ss Corps trying to break into the pocket as well as from the trapped forces who were trying to break out of it and into the open country around Vimoutiers. The drizzle which had been falling all day finally stopped and the evening of Monday 21 August 1944 turned out fine.

Meanwhile other Polish units had been engaged in a drive to Chambois.

It was still not clear who would be near Chambois; it was thought that the Allied troops south of the place might be Americans, although on the other hand they might be Leclerc's 2nd French Armoured Division, but to avoid confusion and to prevent accidents the first Polish tank carried the white over red ensign of Poland as it moved down the 2 km stretch of road from squadron TAC headquarters.

The Polish tank reconnaissance group moved from a small side road on to the highway which connects Trun and Chambois and began the short drive. Round a bend they met head on the leading elements of a German column which had begun to move out of the village. In the fury of the battle which followed not many of the combatants would have noticed that behind them Chambois had been set alight as a result of a fighter-bomber raid carried out by Spitfires and Typhoons and that the dull explosions which marked the progress of the day were German ammunition lorries and petrol tankers blowing up. It was, however, obvious that the Germans still held Chambois in some strength and that they were determined to resist was shown when a grenadier with a panzerfaust destroyed a too adventurous Sherman at close range.

The Polish tanks withdrew, regrouped and were reinforced. Then they came on again under the covering fire of a regiment of artillery. The Cromwells and Shermans drove through the burning streets crunching their way over the debris of tanks, lorries and bodies which littered the entire area and pushed on. In a field just south of the town the first Americans were met and the combined Allies prepared themselves for the battle which would open once the Germans realized that the last escape route had been cut.

It was not until deep into the night that the first serious German attack came in and was driven back by tank guns. Then a second charge was made and driven off and then a third. Unable to break through the village the Germans began a side-step movement hoping to infiltrate through the encirclement and to escape up the slopes of the Mace. But this had been in Allied hands for days and each attempt to thrust past the Polish sentries was driven back.

Out of the darkness there suddenly loomed the huge shapes of Panthers and then a smaller Panzer IV, and behind this a small procession of cars. The first two shots fired at ranges of less than 200 m destroyed the armour and machine guns smashed the staff cars. There was a short interval and then a fresh wave of tanks and infantry swept out of the woods and tried to cross the road. The whole area was dotted with blazing tanks and burning lorries but still the attacks came until, suddenly, there was quiet. The Germans on the Chambois sector had had enough. They would make no more attempts to break out in the Polish area.

It is, perhaps, now time to describe the various German break-out attempts. It will be remembered that the order had been issued that the break-out would take place during the night of 19th/20th and that the break-out areas would be between St Lambert and Chambois.

At 14.30 hrs on the 19th the officer commanding 10th ss Panzer Division arrived in the small village of Villedieu-les-Ballieul for a conference with the GOC 7th Army. During this conference at which the break-out plans were discussed Oberführer Harmel realized for the first time the seriousness of the situation in which not only his own unit was placed but also 5th Panzer and 7th Army. At the divisional Headquarters of 1st ss Division the commanders of the Leibstandarte, the Hitler Youth, and 10th ss worked out the close details of the escape plan, and issued the following orders.

1. Strong enemy tank forces have encircled German troops in the area south of Trun. It is expected that this ring will be strengthened during the

night of the 20th, particularly in the area south east of Trun.

2. The 10th ss will attack on the 20th at 04.00 hrs from the area of Villedieu-Tournai . . . and will break through to Coudehard and Mount Ormel. For this operation two battle groups will be formed. Battle Group 21 will consist of the 21st Panzer Grenadier Regiment and the Pioneer Battalion, while Battle Group 22 will contain 22nd Panzer Grenadier Regiment and the remainder of the Division.

3. The 10th Reconnaissance Battalion will discover the Allied intentions by reconnoitring along the far side of the Chambois–Trun road and will report any usable bridges, particularly those capable of bearing tanks and vehicles, as well as crossing points across the river Dives. Bridgeheads will be formed, beginning at 03.00 hrs, and these will be reinforced by parts of 1st Battalion of 21st Regiment at Chambois and St Lambert and will thereby secure the crossing for the Division.

In view of the shortage of time no firm arrangements could be made to arrange artillery support nor could the battle groups be briefed and collected before the break-out time.

At 03.00 hrs on the 20th the armoured reconnaissance battalion reached the Dives river between St Lambert and Chambois and was there joined by senior officers of other units who joined this larger body. Although it was night there was no let-up in the flow of men and vehicles crossing the river and even the heavy British artillery bombardments did not halt the flow for any length of time. The Luftwaffe was active that night, dropping flares to discover how far the Polish Armoured Division had advanced. Their efforts were not altogether appreciated by the men on the ground: 'Suddenly the sky was lit up by a great white waterfall of light. It was as clear as daylight and how we cursed those flares even though, for once, the Luftwaffe was up bombing the strafing.'

The armoured personnel carriers of 10th ss Division came under fire from Allied tanks as they emerged from a wood just below Villedieu but the Americans had not seen the 88s hidden deeper in the forest and these engaged the US guns in a vicious and protracted duel. The minor battle delayed the advance and it was not until well past sun-up that the main part of the Division was ready to move. Then at St Lambert bridge there was a further hold-up while the ss men removed the dead horses and broken vehicles obstructing the passage of the army.

Once across the bridge the officers of the ss Division and of 116th Panzer Division formed a battle group 'Army Commander', whose task it was to bring out General Hausser. It had been intended to use the gap east of St Lambert through which the 1st ss Panzer Division with the 7th Army Chief of Staff had already escaped but this was found to be completely and firmly occupied by the Allies. It was not, therefore, until early in the afternoon that a new battle group was formed ready to break out and between 15.00 and 16.00 hrs the main strength of the Division crossed the Dives, followed at 17.00 hrs by the sps, flak carriers and signals trucks. The grenadiers waded through the river. By evening the Division had concentrated on the east bank ready for the final rush, but before this could be made the positions held by the Allies on Point 117 had first to be stormed and captured. A small fighting patrol moved out through the gathering darkness and soon flares announced that the road was clear and that the Allies had been forced back. The 10th ss Division broke through.

Others had preceded them but few were to follow in such a mass movement. One group which had left during the darkest part of the night was that under command of 84th Corps. The commander of the Corps, Elfeldt, had already had 85th Division removed from his command and now he was in charge of only 12th ss, the Hitler Youth. This unit, or rather the remnants of it, had had orders to hold the shoulders of the pocket open until the paratroops had forced a passage through which much of the army would escape. Two battle groups were formed, the first, made up of the grenadiers of Krause group together with the headquarters personnel, would follow the paratroops while the motorized battle group would follow the Leibstandarte. Each major unit was then subdivided into smaller groups, each of which would be capable of acting independently of the main body if necessary. All guns for which there were no prime movers, together with all unusable lorries and unnecessary equipment, were to be blown up or set alight. At midnight the grenadiers set off.

The march took the column across country and through a night whose darkness was accentuated by the light of many blazing fires. The firing of useless equipment by the Germans, together with the lorries set alight by Allied air or artillery bombardment, blazed a trail to the narrow corridor through which the entrapped units were filtering. The long August night was filled with noise: the crash of exploding artillery shells and bursts of machine gun fire, the noise of tank tracks and the screams of the men and horses mortally wounded in the unending barrages.

Unless you had been there or had been in a similar situation you cannot understand how severe was the drain upon one's physical and mental powers. A strange neurosis is generated which then is transmitted from man to man. Those of us who had been caught in the same type of situation in Russia recognized the symptoms of 'Kesselfieber' [encirclement fever] and it required the greatest efforts on the part of the officers to overcome it. For as long as one was fighting hard the immediate problems drove out every other consideration, but as soon as there was the possibility of escape then the neuroses began. One manifestation was the spreading of rumours; one such story [supposedly issued by the German forces radio station in Calais] was that air attacks upon the pocket had been or would be called off. Then there was the terrible tiredness, a sort of leaden-footed sensation and, fighting through waves of exhaustion, we would find ourselves still marching, still putting one foot in front of the other and still keeping touch with the man in front and the man behind. There was, I suppose, food but I cannot remember regular meals or even if we ate at all. Just exhaustion so great that at any short halt men would lean against the trees or walls and fall asleep on the spot. And yet each man carried his weapon, ammunition and grenades. We may have been in a serious state but we were not defenceless and in a sense our weapons kept us in touch with reality. There were some units which seemed to move aimlessly about and others which the 'Kesselfieber' had infected so deeply that they were incapable or unwilling to defend themselves. Such formations were an encumbrance; in fact a danger to the rest of us. There were enough non-combatants and headquarters staffs in the fighting zone without adding to their number. During the break-out we were lucky for thick mist covered the ground and we slipped through the trees unseen by the enemy outposts.

The constricted German columns were converging upon the three possible crossing places, all man-made, across the Dives river. These were a stone bridge and a light bridge behind St Lambert and the Moissy ford. At this time during the operation these narrow places were the only remaining crossing points and across them had to pass all the escaping troops. But to reach these the road ran through the village of Tournai-sur-Dives and thus the whole escape route funnelled through a corridor barely 200 m wide. Various attempts were made to construct emergency bridges by driving lorries and tanks into the river bed and planking over these uneven surfaces.

In the sector through which the Leibstandarte was passing there was great congestion on the paths through the woods and columns of vehicles, at points eight lines abreast, ground slowly forward wheel to wheel and nose to tail, guided through the white fog by grenadiers with dimmed pocket torches. By first light the column was west of Chambois where the Leibstandarte panzer were to force a break-through, but the first thrusts were driven back by heavy shell fire. Hitler Youth grenadiers were then ordered to mount the Tigers and to act as an infantry spearhead. From the cover of the woods the panzer and Grenadier group moved forward and into the concentrated barrage fired by the Canadian and Polish guns. In the bed of the Dives river the grenadiers regrouped and formed a screen between Chambois and Trun, that is across the narrow neck of the corridor. Along the length and across the breadth of that bottleneck lay the bodies of those who had been killed while trying to escape.

Wherever one looked there were bodies. The stench was appalling for the fields were filled also with the bodies of artillery horses and civilian cattle. There were columns of burnt out trucks and in the cabs of some the incinerated bodies of the drivers. There were corpses along the roads, in the ditches, some of them blown into the tree tops. Along some stretches of the road whole blocks of lorries formed a dam and had to be pushed to one side by pairs of tanks working together. There could be, under such conditions, no great respect shown to the dead and bodies lying in the roads were often rolled over by the tanks and crushed under the tracks. It was not lack of feeling, but it was more important to save the living than to respect the corpses.

There were quite a number of women dead, particularly in the Horch staff cars and for these one really felt sad. A front line soldier, after all, had death as a constant companion. These women should not have died under such hopeless conditions.

The Hitler Youth grenadier group, now reduced to only 200 men, moved forward from its positions in the woods to the west of the Trun–Chambois road and prepared itself for the final charge. Before them lay the open road swept along its entire length by fixed line machine guns, by tank cannon and by gun-fire. The grenadiers had to pass across this avenue of death without the support of their own armoured fighting vehicles, for they had not been able to cross the Dives river. Although only 10 m wide its steep banks 2 to 3 m high were thus obstacles to tanks, lorries or even horse-drawn transport. The panzer had had to be left behind.

A small Canadian tank and infantry group which had fought its way into St Lambert on Saturday 19th was acting as a cork bottling the neck of the escape route, and to support this group in its difficult task Allied artillery brought down one crashing bombardment after another upon the woods in which the German troops were hiding. Then the armour was brought forward and spaced at 200 m intervals to drive back any attempted escape.

The divisional headquarters was in a farmhouse in the area of La Londe, south west of Trun. Also quartered there was the Tac headquarters of 84th Corps under whose command was the remnant of the Hitler Youth Division. Unforgettable and typical of the situation as it was at that time were the conditions under which the two headquarters were working. In one room of the farmhouse there was a long table on either side of which there were benches without back rests. This room ran the whole length of the house and along one wall was an open chimney. On one side of the table sat Kurt Meyer, the divisional commander and I, his GSO 1. On the other side was General Elfeldt, GOC 84th Corps, and his Chief of Staff, Lieutenant-Colonel von Kriegern.

There were also a few aides-de-camp, runners and drivers, perhaps a dozen in all. We waited throughout the night, alternately dozing off and

153

waking up, expecting reports to come in that the assault by 3rd Para. and by the battle groups had been successful. There was almost no wireless communication.

The 2nd Para. Corps set off at 23.30 hrs on the 19th, but as no report was received by 03.00 hrs on the 20th and as there were no sounds of firing coming from the direction of St Lambert, we assumed that the break-through had been successful. The 12th ss gave the order to follow otherwise the hours of darkness would be too few to allow all the troops to escape.

General Elfeldt and Lieut.-Colonel von Kriegern joined our divisional headquarters group and just before dawn we set out on foot to follow in daylight through the gap which had been made for us. The few remaining vehicles were left behind.

The 84th Corps HQ, without any transport, set off behind a battle group of 12th ss and by daylight on the 20th met a tank unit at St Lambert and was split up. The group reassembled and set out again but east of St Lambert the Corps senior officers hit an enemy outpost and were captured.

Faced with the close-packed Canadian tank and infantry ring the ss grenadiers could take no chance of being involved in a battle, even one of short duration. The whole line would have to charge across the road and battle its way through without pausing to engage or to destroy the enemy.

The first priority was to get out and we gathered ourselves in the thick undergrowth beneath the trees, snaking forwards until along the whole length of the road one could see the tired faces of one's comrades peering out of the bushes, looking and waiting for the signal to cross. As we were so close to the enemy we were not troubled by his artillery fire. I think that perhaps he did not know that we were so near to him for much of the barrage fell a long way behind us and upon a countryside now almost deserted for, remember, we were among the last units to leave.

We gripped our weapons tighter and then came the signal. We may have been tired, even exhausted, but the chance of escape gave us new speed and inspiration. We struck through the Canadian outpost line. We could have taken prisoners but we just disarmed the Tommies and ran on to keep contact with our other groups. When we halted to gain our breath and sheltered in the bushes the word went round that our General, Panzermeyer, had been badly wounded in the head and that he was lying with his face a mask of blood a short way away. That report turned out to be only partly true. A badly stitched head wound had re-opened as he burst across the road and he had been led to safety half blinded by the blood in his eyes. We needed that rest for we had high ground to cross, but once across that crest we were out of the ring. Suddenly we knew that we were through. Once we had escaped we became aware that German artillery shells were landing behind us and to the right and behind us. Then we knew that the relief attempts which we had heard so much about were really happening and that 'Das Reich' was trying to keep the pocket open.

During the 20th some large and organized units managed to escape through the St Lambert–Chambois corridor and there were occasions in which one group would successfully break out without interference while a second group, making its attempt only hours afterwards, would be intercepted and either turned back or destroyed. The Allied troops were still too thin on the ground to form a completely effective cordon and it was not until the late afternoon of the 21st that this was achieved and it could be claimed that the escape of all organized bodies had been totally halted. But on the 20th escape was still possible and there were some interesting stories.

The 353rd Division went through Tournai and then turned eastwards through the briskly burning village. The streets were blocked with traffic and attempts to clear the road slowed down and then halted the progress of the divisional columns. Near the crossing places the divisional commander formed his command into two battle groups and personally reconnoitred the escape routes. Thanks to his careful selection of ground the main body escaped via Moissy while the right-hand assault column broke through west of Chambois. The commander kept a tight hold on his men once out of the encirclement and concentrated them in and around Mount Ormel. His own battle groups were too few in number to form an adequate defence line so he removed from the troops passing through his area all the Para. units and ss men he could muster and with these formed a front facing south-eastwards to hold the Vie sector.

The 3rd Para. Division arrived in its break-out area, but shortly before the break-out time the divisional commander was so badly wounded that command of the unit had to be passed to headquarters of ii Para. Corps. One Para. battle group was formed into small, independent groups and these filtered through the Allied tank line and escaped. It had not been possible to carry out a thorough reconnaissance so that the location of the Canadian and Polish strong points was not known, but the order went out that fighting was to be avoided if possible and that the escape was to take place in total silence. No shot was to be fired. The groups crossed the first bound, slipping through the trees and working their way across open ground, using the cover of every slope or depression to hide them from the Allied tank men. At first light on the 21st they went to ground and stayed hidden in the undergrowth throughout the long hot day and completed their cross-country journey after night fall. The General Officer Commanding 7th Army, Hausser, broke out with the paratroops in the battle Group 'Army Commander', but during the first move he had been badly wounded by having his lower jaw shot away and was finally brought out draped, bleeding but conscious, on the back of a tank.

155

One senior officer of 7th Army Staff, von Gersdorff, who had joined with the headquarters of Panzer Group Eberbach lost contact with the group during the night of the 19th and found himself at dawn on the 20th on the outskirts of St Lambert locked in an immobile vehicle column. Heavy artillery fire had first slowed the column but then the presence of Canadian and Polish tanks halted it completely. Two damaged tanks which had been abandoned by 2nd Panzer Division were dragged forward and these fought down the Canadian anti-tank guns, the Shermans and the Canadian artillery. The road forward was now open and this was the signal for a general advance. A large number of armoured cars, panzer and SP guns emerged from the bushes and undergrowth in which they had been concealed and careered madly across the road. In their charge they hit a unit of the 90th US Division, overran it and captured the Americans. A short distance to the east of the road the Commander ordered a halt to regroup and to count those who had crossed with him. There were representatives from every unit in the pocket and from these a new battle group was formed which carried out a further reconnaissance before forcing its way through the last block to freedom. News of this second break-through spread quickly and when von Gersdorff returned into the pocket to search for 7th Army Commander, he met an unbroken stream of soldiers heading for the gaps which he had made.

On 20 August the 47th Corps, which had already formed battle groups, reached the St Lambert–Chambois sector together with the main strength of 1st SS Panzer Division and that of 2nd Panzer Division. The aggressive actions of the 'Army Commander's Group' had created such alarm in the Canadian line that they had laid down a barrage of an intensity not seen during the whole campaign. Reconnaissance by the 'Leibstandarte SS' showed that the road via Moissy immediately to the north west of Chambois was the one most densely covered with undergrowth and therefore the safest in which to lie concealed. Some small groups used this route and suffered only slight losses but 2nd Panzer fell foul of a strong Allied group and lost heavily. By contrast, 116th Panzer Division, which did not reach the break-out points until the night of 20/21 August, had such an easy passage that they brought no fewer than fifty vehicles out of the encirclement.

A slight mishap cast a shadow over the achievements of that division: one group, which had been defending the southern wing against the Americans since 14 August, did not receive the message ordering its recall to the break-out point and maintained a stubborn defence until it was overrun and taken into captivity.

The Operations Group of 84th Corps, in obedience to orders, had covered the northern wing while the other groups broke out and had protected these against the thrusts by the British and the Canadians. It was the last major headquarters to fight in the pocket and when it left to follow 3rd Para.

Division Elfeldt, the Corps Commander, led his detachments on foot. The unit struck a battle group from 1st Polish Division, was cornered in a narrow lane, surrounded, and taken prisoner after suffering heavy losses. This headquarters, together with that of 84th Division, was the only one of approximately twenty senior command staffs which did not escape from the encirclement.

Those groups which were still in the area of the Dives river on the morning of 20 August took advantage of the II ss Panzer Corps counter-attack. There was a lessening of pressure by the Allied troops which were facing into the pocket as the organized resistance now coming from the ss Corps took effect.

Although it was weak in numbers the counter-attack made several kilometres of ground but, more importantly, it gained a breathing space for those troops still in the pocket and enabled large numbers of infantry to escape together with some panzer and over sixty pieces of artillery.

During the 21st this flow stopped abruptly and permanently. The 9th ss Division was to report that the flow had halted at midday, that is about the time when 53rd Welsh Division had not only linked up with the Canadians at Trun but also with us troops who had arrived in Villedieu-les-Ballieul. Not until the later afternoon was St Lambert finally cleared of the survivors of the German garrison which had been struggling to hold open the crossing points. Patrols from South Alberta Regiment then struck down to Chambois from the village, forming a strong and permanent link with the Poles there.

The ring was now solid and firm, but outside there was one last flicker of life from 9th ss Division under whose command two of the new King Tiger tanks had been placed for testing under active service conditions. The giant machines rolled forward down the Trun road ready to offer battle and to break open the ring, but upon them was poured such a concentration of artillery fire and rockets from the Typhoons still circling above that they were knocked out before they had covered a couple of kilometres. The last trump had been played and had failed.

Aftermath

The battle was over and the whole of the area from the Orne in the west to Mount Ormel in the east and from Falaise in the north to Argentan in the south was one vast cemetery of uninterred dead. Of all that area the largest number had been killed and the greatest amount of damage caused in the sector between Chambois–Trun–Vimoutiers. The Canadian official history reported that the heaviest concentration was south and south west of St Lambert, that is to say, in the area leading up to the escape routes. The acrid smell of burning and burnt-out vehicles was bad but the stomach was turned by the stench of the dead men and horses – and there were thousands of dead horses. The smell was all-pervading and overpowering. So strong in fact that pilots of light artillery observation aircraft flying over the area reported that the stench affected them even hundreds of feet in the air.

Above the battlefield shimmered a miasma of decay and putrefaction; everything was covered with flies and blue-bottles. In the hot August sun the cattle which had been killed only days before were masses of crawling maggots, and the unburied Germans, swollen to elephantine grossness by the hot sun inflating the gases in the stomach, lay with blackened faces in grotesque positions. Here there was no dignity of death. In the worst bombarded areas fragments of bodies festooned the trees and on the Mount Ormel heights an ambulance convoy, hit and destroyed by Typhoons, presented a disgusting spectacle. The immobile wounded had been trapped in the ambulances and had burned to death in so fierce a blaze that their calcined bodies had shrunk to the size of mannikins.

There were whole areas in which one could not pass without treading upon a carpet of the dead. Eisenhower described how it was literally possible to walk for hundreds of yards at a time stepping on nothing but the dead and on decaying flesh. Some roads were completely impassable due to the congestion caused by burned-out trucks, dead horses, smashed tanks and destruction on a scale which the Western Allies had never seen.

Clearing the area was a low priority task and, indeed, some cattle lay rotting until well into November. When it was necessary to clear a congested road then bulldozers were brought in to shovel open large grave areas into which the animal cadavers were pushed and the whole site then covered over. The foetid stench and the rotting bodies were sufficient for the Allies to declare the whole of the area around the Dives river as an 'unhealthy zone' and supplied the civilian population with drinking water brought by convoy from towns as far away as Caen.

It was not until 1961 that the last traces visible to travellers through the area were finally removed, but there are still some signs. Allied tanks form memorials at Mount Ormel and at St Christophe le Jajolet the new bricks in older houses and the pock-marking of shrapnel can still be seen, but it is the countryside itself which remains the most potent memorial. The area is as quiet now as it was before the war came to it, for the valley of the Dives is not a tourist area, but even in its peace it still retains an atmosphere of the horrors which were played out there during the August days of 1944, when two armies were funnelled into and across a few bridges and a ford.

One considers the lie of the land and the few crossing points and then as sudden as a shot in the brain come the questions to which there have been no answers given: why did not the German engineers build bridges across the river so as to increase the number of escape points and why did they not create smoke-screens during daylight hours to hide from Allied aircraft the columns moving out of the pocket? Why was no road kept open leading into the pocket so as to bring forward the badly needed ammunition and the supplies which could have nourished the units holding the walls? There are many questions unanswered; much blame to be apportioned and much praise to be lavished. Some of the unanswered questions were mentioned above; some of the blame has already been laid at the doors of those who were responsible and the praise must go, as it always and rightly should, to the common soldiers and their junior officers, for this was truly a soldiers' battle from beginning to end. The British, the Poles, the French, the Canadians, the Americans – all the Allies fought well, but against that background of carnage and destruction there stands illuminated the ordinary German soldier – infantryman, panzergrenadier and tank man. They never failed to do their duty in conditions which were, particularly towards the end, no less than apocalyptic. Much of their sacrifice would not have been necessary had the generals who commanded them shown the same courage in confronting Hitler as did the simple soldier in facing tanks, guns, air assault, hunger, thirst and privation. The generals failed their men and the 10,000 German dead of the Falaise pocket were the price of their failure.

It was over. Behind the thin screen of ss grenadiers, paratroopers and Army units which the 353rd Division had formed, the miscellaneous groups which had escaped encirclement began to move towards the Seine, closely pursued by soldiers who were no less exhausted than the Germans but in whose nostrils there was the heady scent of victory.

The Seine was neither a refuge nor a barrier against the energetic tank thrusts of the Allied armour, but for an all too brief period, so far as the

Germans were concerned, there was a momentary lessening of the tension – a breathing space in which the losses of the Normandy campaign could be totalled. One German historian estimated that only 20,000 men of the 80,000 in the pocket managed to escape, that a further 50,000 were taken prisoner and that 10,000 died on the field of battle. The American registration unit which carried out investigations in those sectors in which only US troops had fought reported that it found 220 tanks, 160 SP guns, more than 700 pieces of artillery and 5,000 vehicles. British investigators of an Operational Research Team carrying out a similar exercise in the British, Canadian and Polish areas reported that in that sector there were 187 armoured fighting vehicles and SP guns, 157 armoured cars or personnel carriers, 1,800 lorries, 669 civilian cars or staff vehicles and 252 pieces of ordnance. Neither team reported on the number of horse-drawn carts which were found or tried to estimate the number of dead animals.

The losses suffered by the Hitler Youth Division were shocking. The divisional commander, Panzermeyer, calculated that he lost 80 per cent of his Grenadiers, the same percentage of his tanks, 70 per cent of the divisional reconnaissance and personnel carriers, 60 per cent of the artillery and 50 per cent of the soft-skinned vehicles.

The German troops lost in the pocket could have been used to halt the further advances of 3rd US Army towards the Seine, had they been withdrawn in time. But they were destroyed piecemeal and while they were suffering and dying American armoured columns, brushing aside the weak opposition which faced them in the heartland of France, captured Paris on 25 August. Four days later the last German troops had crossed the Seine, as Matthew Cooper points out in his work on the German Army, skilfully led by commanders who prevented the retreat from becoming a rout. And this despite losses in equipment on an unbelievable scale. Between one hundred and one hundred and twenty armoured fighting vehicles were brought across the Seine; 2,200 had been destroyed or abandoned in Normandy. Fifty Divisions had been committed to action during June. Now only ten could be classed as fighting units. In three months the battle of Normandy had cost the Germans almost twice as many men as had the fighting in Stalingrad.

It is easy to blame Hitler for all the mistakes and there can be no doubt that the military ability of the Supreme Commander had been shown to be faulty, but the early chapters of this book have also shown how differences in opinion among the senior German field commanders, their deeply laid habits of unquestioning obedience to authority and the fact that many had been compromised by association with the 20 July bomb plotters, led to them fighting battles or accepting orders to undertake offensives for which there was no hope of victory and every probability of utter defeat.

Guderian describes exactly the results of the High Command attitude.

While our panzer units still existed our leaders had chosen to fight a static battle in Normandy. Now that our motorized forces have been squandered and destroyed they were compelled to fight the mobile battle that they had hitherto refused to face. Favourable chances that the boldness of the American Command occasionally offered us we were no longer in a position to exploit. The original intention – to counter-attack the southern wing of the advancing Americans – had to be given up.

It was clear that the German Army in the West was not about to face total disaster, it was already experiencing it, and there was no reason why the war could not be brought to an end in September. Generals Blumentritt and Zimmermann, in answers to questions raised during an interrogation and dealing with this phase of operations on the Western front, stated that by the end of August and the beginning of September the situation facing the German Army in the West was critical.

The two Army Groups 'B' and 'G' had been torn wide open on their inner flanks and the danger existed that the mass of Army Group 'G' would be caught in the valley of the Rhone and crushed against the plateau of the Langres. Similarly Army Group 'B' had been split in the centre and the 5th Panzer Army, holding that sector, had been as good as annihilated. The 15th Army on the right was threatened with encirclement while 1st Army, on the left, was being pressed back eastwards and had been flung back towards Luxembourg and the Ardennes.

The way to the Ruhr and to the heart of Germany lay open, so far as they were concerned, to any commander who had sufficient forces and was bold enough to risk a decisive thrust. Operation Market Garden, Montgomery's imaginative thrust to lay a 90 km long airborne carpet, provided such an opportunity and with its failure there died the chance to have capitalized upon the victories which had been won in a single month, in August 1944, in and around Falaise.

3

APPENDIXES
BIBLIOGRAPHY
AND INDEX

Appendix 1

The Allied Command Structure and Order of Battle in Western Europe from 6 June to 22 August 1944

FRANKLIN D. ROOSEVELT
President
and Commander in Chief of the US Armed Forces

WINSTON S. CHURCHILL
Prime Minister
and British Minister of Defence

THE COMBINED CHIEFS OF STAFF

US Joint Chiefs of Staff
Admiral Leahy
General Marshall
Admiral King
Lieut.-Gen. Arnold

British Chiefs of Staff
General Alan Brooke
Admiral Cunningham
Air Chief Marshal Portal
Lieut.-Gen. Hastings Ismay
Field Marshal Dill

SUPREME HEADQUARTERS ALLIED
EXPEDITIONARY FORCE
General Eisenhower – Supreme Commander
Air Chief Marshal Tedder – Deputy
Lieut.-Gen. Bedell Smith – Chief of Staff

Lieut.-Gen. Bradley
Commander 1st US Army 10 Mar. – 1 Aug 1944
Commander 12th US Army Group
1 Aug. 1944–8 May 1945

General Montgomery
Commander 21st Army Group 10 Mar. 1944
Allied Ground Forces Commander
10 Mar. 1944–1 Sept. 1944

Lieut.-Gen. Hodges
Commander 1st US Army

Lieut.-Gen. Dempsey
Commander 2nd Army

Lieut.-Gen. Patton
Commander 3rd US Army

Lieut.-Gen. Crerar
Commander 1st Canadian Army

Total forces under command from 6 June–22
Aug. 1944
7 Corps: 6 US armoured divisions, 1 Free French
armoured division, 14 US infantry divisions, and
2 US airborne divisions

Total forces under command from 6 June–22
Aug. 1944
4 British and 1 Canadian Corps; 3 British armoured divisions, 1 Canadian and 1 Polish armoured
division, 8 British and 2 Canadian infantry divisions, 2 airborne divisions (1 held in the UK)

Commander in Chief Allied Naval Forces
Admiral Ramsay

Western Task Force
Rear Admiral Kirk USN

Eastern Task Force
Rear Admiral Vian RN

Coastal Command
Air Marshal Sholto Douglas

Allied Expeditionary Air Force
Air Chief Marshal Leigh-Mallory

Advanced Allied Expeditionary Force
Air Marshal Coningham

2nd Tactical Air Force
Air Marshal Coningham

Allied Strategic Air Force
Bomber Command
Air Marshal Harris
8th USAAF
Lieut.-Gen. Doolittle

Notes:

The Naval forces available on D-Day were: 3 RN and 3 USN battleships, 17 RN, 3 USN, 2 Free French and 1 Polish cruiser. 2 RN Monitors, 3 RN HQ and 2 USN HQ ships. 66 RN and RCN, 30 USN, 2 Polish, 3 Norwegian and 1 Free French destroyers. 11 RN, 2 USN, 4 Free French frigates. 17 RN, 2 Free French and 2 Greek corvettes. 17 USN patrol boats, 4 RN and 2 Dutch sloops, 30 RN armed trawlers, 88 RN and RCN minesweepers and 9 US minesweepers, together with 4,126 landing craft, 736 ancillary ships and 864 merchant ships.

The aircraft available on D-Day were: Coastal Command, 1,030 RAF and 40 USAAF; Allied Strategic Air Force, 1,470 RAF bombers, 1,970 USAAF bombers 130 RAF light bombers. Air Defence of Great Britain, 2nd Tactical Air Force, 9th Air Force, Airborne and Transport Operations: 100 medium and light RAF bombers, 1,400 RAF fighters and fighter/bombers, 490 RAF night fighters, 460 RAF troop carriers and transports, 350 RAF reconnaissance aircraft and 80 air/sea rescue aircraft. 700 USAAF medium and light bombers, 2,300 USAAF fighters and fighter/bombers, 900 USAAF troop carriers and transports and 170 reconnaissance aircraft. 3,500 Allied troop-carrying gliders.

Not itemized under the Army's strength are the 8 independent tank and armoured brigades in 21st Army Group, the 79th Armoured Division which never operated as such, deploying its 3 regiments of AVRE's, flail tanks and flame throwers in usually squadron strength. There were also 2 Special Service (Commando) Brigades, 2 SAS regiments, 2 Free French parachute battalions, 1 Belgian and Dutch infantry Brigade, 6 AGRA's, 1 Czech Independent armoured brigade (in the United Kingdom throughout the Normandy campaign), 8 heavy anti-aircraft brigades and L of C troops. Similarly the US order of battle does not include independent artillery brigades, mechanized cavalry groups, tank destroyer units and Ranger battalions.

Appendix 2

The German Command Structure and Order of Battle in Western Europe from 6 June to 22 August 1944

ADOLF HITLER
Supreme Commander of the Armed Forces
and German Chancellor

OBERKOMMANDO DER WEHRMACHT (OKW)
Chief: **Field Marshal Keitel**
Chief of Operations Staff: **General Jodl**
Deputy Chief of Operations Staff: **General Warlimont**

Commander in Chief: West
Field Marshal von Rundstedt to 2 July 1944
Field Marshal von Kluge 2 July–17 Aug. 1944
Field Marshal Model 17 Aug.–5 Sept. 1944

(4 Panzer and Panzergrenadier Divisions in OKW reserve on D-Day)

High Command Navy (OKM)
Grand Admiral Doenitz

Naval Group West
Vice-Admiral Krancke
5 destroyers
6 torpedo boats
35 'S' boats
500 (c) patrol boats and minesweepers
40 U-boats available for operations in the Channel and in the Bay of Biscay.
(at his disposal on D-Day)

High Command Luftwaffe (OKL)
Reichsmarschall Goering

3rd Air Fleet
Field Marshal Sperrle
402 bombers
336 fighters
89 reconnaissance aircraft
64 transport aircraft
(at his disposal on 31 May 1944)

Army Group 'G'
General Blaskowitz
(3 panzer divisions in reserve on D-Day)

Army Group 'B'
Field Marshal Rommel to 17 July 1944
Field Marshal von Kluge 17 July–17 Aug. 1944
Field Marshal Model 17 Aug. 1944–Apr. 1945
(3 panzer divisions in reserve on D-Day)

Panzer Group West
(subsequently became 5th Panzer Army on 6 Aug. 1944)
General Geyr von Schweppenburg to 5 July 1944
General Eberbach 4 July–9 Aug. 1944
General of the Waffen ss Dietrich

1st Army
General von der Chevallerie to 5 Sept. 1944
4 infantry divisions formed into two corps as at D-Day

19th Army
General von Sodenstern
7 infantry divisions and a Luftwaffe field corps as at D-Day

Armed Forces Netherlands Command
General Christiansen
2 infantry divisions and 1 Luftwaffe field division as at D-Day

15th Army
General von Salmuth to 25 Aug. 1944
15 infantry divisions, 3 Luftwaffe field divisions as at D-Day

7th Army
General Dollmann (died 28 June 1944)
General of the Waffen ss Hausser 29 June–20 Aug. 1944
General Eberbach 20 Aug.–31 Aug. 1944
12 infantry divisions and 2 Para. divisions in 3 Corps and a Para. Corps as at D-Day

Notes:

The Ration Strength of the German Armed Forces on 1 March 1944 was: 806,927 Army; 337,140 Luftwaffe (total includes flak gunners and paratroops who came under Luftwaffe authority); 96,084 Kriegsmarine; 85,230 ss and police; 61,439 foreign volunteers; 13,631 others. Total 1,400,451 plus 145,611 'Armed Forces Auxiliaries'.

Appendix 3

HQ Staff Army Group 'B', 31 July 1944

This week witnessed the large-scale attack by 1st US Army, apparently reinforced by elements of 3rd US Army. On Panzer Group West sector the enemy made attempts on 25 and 26 July with two Canadian infantry Divisions and an armoured brigade to penetrate between Bourguebus and the Orne on a front 7 km in width . . . On the 30th the enemy attacked the western flank of Panzer Group West and penetrated to a depth of 5 km . . .

On 7th Army front the anticipated major assault by the enemy commenced on 24 July . . . the enemy succeeded in penetrating the front between Vire and the sea. Our losses in men and material due to the superiority of the enemy's air forces and artillery are so high that it was impossible to form a strong defensive front very quickly. The main attack between the Army boundary and Percy could be held but the situation between St Hilaire and Percy to the sea has still not been clarified and powerful enemy forces are being ferried towards the gap . . .

Enemy intentions: . . . The British and American forces will first attempt to extend their lodgement area southwards using the bulk of their armies, and once the break-through has been successfully achieved will make a thrust towards Paris.

7 August 1944

. . . The enemy moreover appears to intend a thrust towards Paris. To do this he is endeavouring, with the British forces, to gain the area around Falaise and using the US forces to outflank 7th Army from the west and to reach the Le Mans area.

The British forces will moreover continue their attempts to break through at Vire, but the disposition of their forces east of the Orne . . . provides grounds for believing that there will be a north–south thrust from this area with the object of achieving a double outflanking movement.

Part of the American forces is committed to the projected sealing off and occupation of Brittany . . .

The 5th Panzer Army and 7th Army . . . have caused his [the enemy's] first operational plan to fail. It is only recently that the enemy has succeeded in breaking through to Cotentin and thus on the west flank is approaching at last his first objectives, reaching the line Domfront–Avranches and of sealing off Brittany.

All possible units of Army Group 'B' have been brought up to the battle front, the armoured formations have been assembled on the western flank of 7th Army, and with these an east–west thrust has been made on Avranches to cut off the enemy at Cotentin and to make it impossible for him to continue his operations in the south.

Army Group 'B' to OKW, 11 August 1944

Ref.: Result of conversations with the Army Group Commanders.

ss Colonel General Hausser was still of the opinion that the offensive towards Avranches was still practical, once regrouping had taken place, but his opinion has changed. He now considers that this operation is no longer practicable since the enemy has brought forward fresh forces which . . . can no longer be overcome. The drive to the sea cannot be quickly carried out but will be a hard and a long battle. The German panzer forces are no longer equal to this task.

Thus both c.-in-c.s are of the same opinion.

I agree with that standpoint and note, in addition, that the situation on the deep southern flank has become rapidly more acute now that the enemy has turned northwards.

. . . In order to restore the situation strong panzer forces must be thrown in without delay and the following units . . . can be made available if the Mortain salient is shortened. This, in effect, means the abandonment of the idea of a break-through to the sea.

From Army Group 'B', 10 August 1944

The American force with one tank division, 3 infantry divisions and 2 light motorized formations has advanced into the southern flank of Army Group and has taken possession of the region from Le Mans to the east. He has now turned to the line Mayenne–Beaumont-Bonntable–La Forte Bernard, i.e. to the north.

It appears that he is striving for a double encirclement of 5th Panzer and 7th Armies in co-operation with the continuing thrust of the British towards Falaise. One characteristic of the offensive is the employment of large fighter and bomber formations . . .

Infantry Corps are not in a position to guarantee the defence of the southern flank and to keep open the Alençon–Flers highway which is essential for our supply service.

It should be considered whether a short but well-directed panzer thrust might not destroy the enemy offensive spearheads which are thrusting northwards, in order to establish a basis for the successful prosecution of the decisive offensive. These formations can be withdrawn temporarily from the Mortain area . . .

Favourable weather conditions for the enemy and the time required to bring our troops forward make it likely that the attack on Avranches will not be launched before 20 August . . .

From GOC Army Group 'B', 12 August 1944

Ref.: The Top Secret order for Army Chiefs signed Adolf Hitler, dated 11 August.

The Führer has decreed that the serious threat to the deep southern flank of Army Group 'B' requires that it be eliminated by an offensive.

1. The 15th US Corps in the Le Mans region and extending to Alençon must be smashed by a concentrated attack. The enemy attacking in the Alençon–Mamers direction will be struck in the flank by a panzer force along the line Sille–Guillaume–Beaumont. As soon as 9th Panzer becomes free it will join this offensive. General der Panzer Truppen Eberbach will be GOC.

2. In order to free troops for this offensive 7th Army will release forces and send them southwards. I am in agreement with a shortening of the line between Sourdeval and Mortain in order to make troops available . . . The decisive areas are Falaise and Mortain.

3. . . . troops being built up around Chartres will cover Paris and the rear of Army Group 'B'. These troops must be sent without delay to mop up after Eberbach's group. Anti-tank troops . . . are to rush forward along the main roads to halt enemy armoured reconnaissance in the direction of Paris.

4. After the successful operation against 15th US Corps the offensive to reach the sea must be resumed.

SECRET

HQ Staff Army Group, 14 August 1944

Weekly Situation Report

The enemy has at present in France about 50 Divisions and powerful GHQ troops. A further 31 divisions are available in Great Britain and more are in the USA. The transport of troops across the Channel continues at an increased rate.

The enemy's main objective, while maintaining his frontal attacks to achieve a break-through, is to outflank and encircle the main part of 5th Panzer Army and 7th Army, on both flanks. The southern outflanking group

(15th US Corps and probably also the 20th Corps which is moving up) has crossed the Mortagne–Alençon line and has swung westwards, after having first moved east and north. The intention is to drive at the rear of 7th Army or to engage our panzer forces which are being brought up. In this connection a large-scale enemy attack east of the Orne is to be expected. Not until he has dealt with the 5th Panzer and 7th Army is the enemy expected to embark on further operations. This is confirmed by the fact that he is only feeling his way forward with reconnaissance troops east from the area of Le Mans.

American Army units, reinforced by French resistance groups, are tied down in Brittany in battles for the fortresses there.

The transfer to Normandy of the Supreme Command of the Allied invasion forces affords fresh proof that a second, large-scale landing upon the west coast of Europe is not anticipated. On the other hand, the possibility of a large-scale airborne landing by troops stationed in England against the Army Group cannot be discounted.

Army Group 'B' will assemble the bulk of the panzer formations on the south-eastern flank under General der Panzer Truppen Eberbach, and then destroy the enemy in the Alençon area.

Notes:

As a result of increased enemy air activity, supplies to all sectors of the battle line have become difficult. This lack of mobility continues to exert a hampering effect upon our operations.

Since 6 June Army and SS formations have
destroyed: 3,370 tanks
               475 aircraft

Our losses since 6 June and up to 13 August 1944
are: 3,630 officers
   151,487 NCOs and men
     3,813 Russians
   ————
   158,930

Replacements received total: 30,069 men
Replacements en route: 9,933 men

Signature

Bibliography

Barnet, Corelli. *The British Army*. Allen Lane.

Bielefeld and Essame. *The Battle for Normandy*. B. T. Batsford.

Blumenson, M. *Breakout and Pursuit*. Dept. of US Army.

Buganski, W. *Poles in the Battle of Western Europe*. Warsaw.

Cave-Brown, Anthony. *Bodyguard of Lies*. W. H. Allen

Cooper, M. *The German Army*. Macdonald & Janes.

Criegern, A. von. *Die Kämpfe des 84 Armee Korps von 6/6 bis 20/8/1944*. Unpublished.

Darby and Cunliffe. *A Short History of 21st Army Group*. Gale & Polden.

Ellis, L. F. *Victory in the West*. Vol. 1. HMSO.

Florentin, E. *The Battle of the Falaise Gap*. Paris.

Garganico, W. *86te Armee Korps*. Unpublished.

Harzer, W. *Die 9te SS Division im Westen*. Unpublished.

HQ 2nd Army. *History of Operations 2nd Army*. Bielefeld.

Hayn, W. *Die Invasion: Von Cotentin bis Falaise*. Vowinckel Verlag.

Herrmann, C. H. *Die 9te Panzer Division*. Podzun Verlag.

Jackson, C. *Operations of 8th Corps*. BAOR.

Lewin, Ronald. *Montgomery as Military Commander*. B. T. Batsford.

Macksey, Kenneth. *Crucible of Power: The Fight for Tunisia 1942–1943*. Hutchinson.

Meyer, Kurt. *Grenadiere*. Schild Verlag.

Mikce, Alexander. *Caen: Anvil of Victory*. Souvenir Press.

Orde, Boden. *The Household Cavalry at War: The Story of the Second Household Cavalry Regiment*. Gale and Polden, Aldershot.

Randel. A Short History of 30 Corps. Bünde.

Ramsay, W. After the Battle. No. 8. Battle of Britain Prints.

Schuster, K. *Die Aufstellung und Einsatz der 85te Inf. Division im Westen*. Unpublished.

Tessin, G. *Verbände und Truppen der deutschen Wehrmacht und Waffen* SS. *1939–1945*. Biblio Verlag, Osnabruck.

Tieke. *Im Feuersturm letzter Kriegsjahre*. II SS Panzer Korps; 9te und 10te SS *Panzer Divisionen*. Munin Verlag.

Wilmot, Chester. *Struggle for Europe*. Collins.

Zimmerman. *Oberbefehlshaber West in the Normandy campaign*. Unpublished.

7te Armee Kriegstagebuch. Unpublished.

81ste Armee Korps. Unpublished.

276te Division. Unpublished.

277te Division. Unpublished.

Panzer Armee Oberkommando 5. Unpublished.

88te Armee Korps. Kriegstagebuch. Unpublished.

Index